Virtual K–8 Teaching

Virtual K–8 Teaching

A Handbook for Building Productive Teacher-Student Relationships

Nicholas M. Baker

ROWMAN & LITTLEFIELD
Lanham • Boulder • New York • London

Published by Rowman & Littlefield
An imprint of The Rowman & Littlefield Publishing Group, Inc.
4501 Forbes Boulevard, Suite 200, Lanham, Maryland 20706
www.rowman.com

86-90 Paul Street, London EC2A 4NE, United Kingdom

Copyright © 2023 by Nicholas M. Baker

All rights reserved. No part of this book may be reproduced in any form or by any electronic or mechanical means, including information storage and retrieval systems, without written permission from the publisher, except by a reviewer who may quote passages in a review.

British Library Cataloguing in Publication Information Available

Library of Congress Cataloging-in-Publication Data

Names: Baker, Nicholas M., 1973– author.
Title: Virtual K–8 teaching : A handbook for building productive teacher-student relationships / Nicholas M. Baker.
Description: Lanham : Rowman & Littlefield, [2023] | Includes bibliographical references. | Summary: "Handbook for Virtual K–8 Teachers is a deep dive into the ways in which virtual K–8 teachers build those ever-elusive relationships with virtual students"—Provided by publisher.
Identifiers: LCCN 2023002504 (print) | LCCN 2023002505 (ebook) | ISBN 9781475871098 (cloth) | ISBN 9781475871104 (paperback) | ISBN 9781475871111 (epub)
Subjects: LCSH: Web-based instruction—United States—Handbooks, manuals, etc. | Education, Elementary—United States—Computer-assisted instruction—Handbooks, manuals, etc. | Teacher-student relationships—United States—Handbooks, manuals, etc.
Classification: LCC LB1028.57 .B35 2023 (print) | LCC LB1028.57 (ebook) | DDC 371.33/44678—dc23/eng/20230313
LC record available at https://lccn.loc.gov/2023002504
LC ebook record available at https://lccn.loc.gov/2023002505

To my wife, Marina, and my little girl, Violetta, for your love and patience during this process. I love you both!

Contents

Preface	ix
Introduction	xi
Chapter 1: Participants	1
Chapter 2: Student Engagement	11
Chapter 3: Transactional Distance	23
Chapter 4: Teacher Presence	41
Chapter 5: Student Sense of Belonging	77
Chapter 6: The Educational Community	99
Chapter 7: Literature on the Virtual Classroom in K–12 Settings	109
Chapter 8: That One Student	111
Conclusion	121
Appendix A: Participant Recruitment: Virtual Middle-School Teachers	125
Bibliography	127
About the Author	135

Preface

My name is Nick Baker. As I write this, I have completed 23 years of teaching. I taught sixth grade for 3 years in a brick-and-mortar setting in rural Illinois and have now completed my 20th year of virtual teaching in a K–8 classroom in southern California. I will primarily focus on my virtual teaching here, though many of the concepts discussed pertain to brick-and-mortar and hybrid settings as well.

Throughout my years of virtual teaching, I have worked with families of students from each grade in K–8. In fact, through the first few years of virtual teaching, I taught students from each K–8 grade in my classroom, simultaneously, each year. This meant that I sometimes worked with a family who had three or four students enrolled in my school, the Violetta Virtual Academies (VIVA), who were each assigned to my class list. Later, things were streamlined to allow each teacher to work with only one grade level per year. I eventually landed on teaching only sixth grade. However, those first few years gave me an important glimpse into the reality that is the full spectrum of K–8 virtual teaching and learning.

Those years also granted me a look at the gamut of differing home-schooling realities, student needs, and what it is for teachers to prepare lessons in the virtual K–8 world. Most importantly, I have learned that the building of productive and meaningful teacher-student relationships in the virtual environment is both the most important piece of the virtual teaching puzzle and, often, the most difficult to achieve.

Although I have learned many things from my experience, I do not claim to know it all. That's impossible. Much of what I have learned has been a product of my collaboration with amazing teaching teams at VIVA. I continue to listen and learn each year, contributing where I may be helpful. Comparing notes with colleagues has solidified my view that the most important piece of the virtual teaching equation has consistently been the cruciality of the building of productive and meaningful teacher-student relationships. In fact, this concept was so important to me that when I was finishing my doctoral degree,

I chose to focus on the building of meaningful and productive teacher-student relationships in virtual middle school settings as the topic for my dissertation. I graduated in July 2021 with a doctoral degree in Curriculum, Teaching and Learning Leadership from Northeastern University in Boston. . . . and yes, as I live in southern California, and my university was in Boston, my degree was largely completed . . . you guessed it! Virtually!

Introduction

"Kids don't care how much you know, until they know you care." These words have been attributed to author and educator, John C. Maxwell, to President Theodore Roosevelt and to a few others. Regardless of its origin, it is my opinion that in terms of establishing the teacher-student relationship, truer words have never been spoken. Although this quote is applicable to nearly any teaching environment, the student perception of teacher care is an especially crucial element in the virtual classroom. We can safely assume that not Maxwell, Roosevelt, or, for that matter, the other possible contributors to the quote had considered virtual middle school teaching when uttering those words. However, this quote is more significant than ever to the virtual K–12 setting.

In this book, I will provide theory and reasoning from the literature utilized in my doctoral studies, as well as practical, concrete suggestions that you can use in your virtual (or brick-and-mortar) classroom tomorrow or later today, depending on when you read this. I obtained much of this information through discussions with the eight Violetta Virtual Academy (VIVA) middle school teachers I interviewed for my dissertation. Some information presented here will come from my experience and some will come from collaborative discussions throughout each of my 20 years of virtual K–8 teaching.

It is true that many of the duties and responsibilities of the virtual middle school teacher are, at times, familiar to all teachers, regardless of educational model. Still, a great deal of the job is unfamiliar, uncharted territory to those teachers working in traditional brick-and-mortar school settings. Issues such as student engagement, teacher presence, and student sense of belonging are critical to all school models. However, the manner in which each of these issues is addressed is quite different in the virtual setting than it is in the brick-and-mortar. Physical proximity to students and the ability to readily communicate throughout the day are challenges that are specific to the virtual setting.

The challenges of teaching virtually became universally known when the COVID-19 pandemic altered the ways in which traditional schools functioned. As brick-and-mortar schools scrambled to emulate the feel of an in-person school, virtually, virtual schools did not have to change operations all that much, aside from keeping up with demand and creating wait lists for prospective students. This explosion of new enrollees that had been precipitated by the pandemic and by the inability of brick-and-mortar schools to effectively adjust to the virtual school setting was, indeed, a challenge.

How does a virtual teacher establish teacher presence, both academic and social? How does a virtual teacher facilitate the opportunity for student engagement? How does a virtual teacher foster students' sense of belonging? This book will examine the challenges that face virtual middle school teachers as they work to build meaningful and productive teacher-student relationships in virtual environments with little to no in-person communication. Solutions to these challenges will be offered as theory is discussed and tips and tricks from current virtual teachers are presented.

Again, while I do not now, nor ever will, know it all, I have accumulated quite a bit of information, as well as tips and tricks. I was also awarded the National Coalition for Public School Options California Pioneer Teacher of the Year in 2009. This honor was thanks to multiple student nominations, as well as one colleague nomination. I was humbled. But I also realized that it was incumbent on me to live up to the standard implied in the title of the award. Being recognized as a pioneer meant staying on top of current trends and technology utilized in virtual teaching. However, there is always new technology, a new online teaching tool, a new game, and so on. Some are great, and some, well, not so much. From the time I started writing this sentence to now, there are probably three new educational programs that have launched online. It is hard to be completely cognizant of all things in virtual education. . . . and that's ok. No matter what technology is available, a great deal of student success comes down to a teacher's human interaction with students. Obviously, technology and online tools play a large role in virtual learning, but the human element is irreplaceable.

In my studies, I was able to identify five areas of teaching that are absolutely crucial to effective virtual teaching and building connections with virtual students. Those areas are transactional distance, teaching presence, student engagement, student sense of belonging, and educational community. So, let's start helping you build those meaningful and productive teacher-student relationships that will help students succeed.

Each of the participants in this study is a middle school teacher at VIVA (e.g., Appendix). In selecting the participants, the teachers chosen for this study each needed to satisfy the following criteria. Each of the educators needed to have taught in both brick-and-mortar and virtual classroom settings. They have each taught at VIVA for at least 3 years. The participants should have been virtual students at some point in their academic careers, although this was not a requirement. Having been a virtual student was true of all but one of the participants, Daisy, who had never learned in the virtual environment. The other seven participants had, at one time, been virtual students, with all this virtual experience coming in college and not during K–12 education. The names of the participants have been changed to ensure anonymity. Of the eight participants, Michelle, Mike, and Daisy are sixth grade teachers; Karen, Tammy, Joy, and Bobbi are eighth grade teachers; and Jill is the sole seventh grade teacher.

The analysis of the discussions with the participants in this study yielded five themes and 11 subthemes. The themes that emerged were (1) deliberate teacher presence is necessary in the virtual environment, (2) teacher fostering of student sense of belonging in the virtual environment, (3) a recognition of the reality of the significant transactional distance found in the virtual environment, (4) the crucial elements of the virtual educational community, and (5) that one student the teachers could not forget. These themes represent common threads found among the transcripts of the eight middle school teachers who were interviewed for this study. The themes are interconnected, as they each signify a piece of the study's greater purpose, which is the building of meaningful teacher-student relationships in the virtual middle school environment.

A NOTE ABOUT THE "FROM THE PD!" SECTIONS

Over my years at VIVA, I have helped with the occasional professional development session. Recently, I presented my dissertation findings to my fellow teachers and to the administration. My goal in presenting is to share something useful with those attending, while simultaneously learning from them. Our team is awesome. We happily share information freely. I learn from my fellow teachers, and they, hopefully, learn from me.

I will include a transcript from the chat of a recent professional development that I presented. I asked the teachers to respond to my questions in the chat. I have removed all the names and left only the answers. The reason I am including this is because I believe it could be helpful to you, the reader. For this example, I was presenting to slightly more than 100 teachers. When answers were redundant, I mostly removed duplicates.

The chats at the end of the chapters give several real-world examples of teachers utilizing the big ideas of this study to allow for opportunities for engagement. You, the reader, can implement many of these ideas tomorrow or later today. That, to me as a teacher, is gold. I know I stole some of these ideas almost immediately. Pet parade? Yeah! Let's do that! Also, the chat serves as a reminder that although a teacher may feel as though they are not getting through to a student, that might not necessarily be the case.

INTRODUCTION TO THE STUDY

Over the past 20 years in the US, online education has grown significantly. Virtual K–12 school enrollments increased by more than 2,000 students between the 2016–2017 and the 2017–2018 school years. During this time, students enrolling in blended learning environments rose by more than 16,000 students, and 39 states boasted either virtual or blended schools.[1] Each year, the number of K–12 students enrolled in virtual classes increases, as does the need for well-trained virtual K–12 teachers.

While the virtual educational model has filled a specific need for many students, questions have arisen regarding the challenges of building teacher-student relationships in an environment that sees little to no in-person contact between teachers and students. Teacher-student interaction is particularly significant in the K–12 virtual environment.[2] Thus, teacher-student relationships need to be deliberately nurtured, especially in the virtual classroom environment. Clearly, when teachers and students do not see each other in-person, every day, the fostering of such relationships may become more challenging, as Toppin & Toppin[3] observed, when they shared:

> From the outside looking in, it would appear as if being a virtual teacher is not very challenging. Yet, to be an effective virtual teacher, nothing can be further from the truth. Virtual teachers are just as confronted by the need to engage their students in meaningful curricula activities as are their face-to-face counterparts. However, because they are in a virtual setting, they quite often do not get the same level of support. (p. 1576)

Due to the challenging nature of building strong teacher-student relationships in virtual environments, it is crucial that teachers in virtual settings prioritize and specifically plan for the building of teacher-student connections.[4]

When I set out to study the concept of the ways in which virtual middle school teachers build meaningful and productive relationships with their virtual students, I made a deliberate decision to utilize the narrative inquiry theoretical framework. Narrative inquiry is a framework that allows participants in a study to tell their stories while answering open-ended questions. This was important to me, as the narrative inquiry research model afforded me the opportunity to learn from the stories of the teachers servicing students in virtual environments. I was able to get out of the way and allow teachers to tell their own stories while limiting my bias toward the subject. Meaning was ultimately made from the storytelling of the participants. This meaning created the data that was utilized in this study.

The Number of Virtual Classrooms Has Grown

To understand the significance of teacher-student relationships in virtual settings, it is necessary to first discuss the great number of teachers and students operating in this environment. At least five million K–12 students in America have taken at least one virtual class.[5] During the 2013–2014 school year, roughly 300,000 US K–12 students were enrolled in full-time online schools, with five states requiring students to take at least one online course.[6] One of the largest American providers of virtual K–12 education in the US is K12 Inc (now Stride). As of 2015, K12 Inc.'s schools enrolled at least 100,000 K–12 students.[7] In the 2017–2018 school year, 501 full-time virtual schools enrolled 297,712 students, while 300 blended American schools enrolled 132,960 students.[8] Admissions into virtual schools grew by more than 2,000 students between 2016–2017 and 2017–2018. During this same time, enrollments in blended learning schools increased by slightly more than 16,000 students.[9] As of 2021, K12 Inc (Stride) has boasted the enrollment of one million virtual K–12 students in America, while VIVA, the school at the center of study in this research, claims to currently, at the time of my writing, enroll 17,000 students.[10] K12's claim of one million students includes those students enrolled in virtual academies around the US, as well as those families who have chosen to buy the curriculum to homeschool their children without the structure of a virtual academy. Given the numbers, K–12 virtual schooling has shown itself to be a consequential player in today's overall educational environment.

The COVID-19 Effect

While this study began well before the COVID-19 pandemic, COVID-19 has affected the ways in which children attend school globally and needs to be addressed here. As of March 2020, 1.5 billion students worldwide had been educationally displaced due to the pandemic.[11] As this worldwide health event has affected the education of such a great number of people, it would be negligent to not mention COVID-19 in this study.

When COVID-19 began to be viewed as a serious threat to health, and due to the unknown nature of the communicability of the virus, many schools put into action mitigation measures in hopes of reducing the number of infections. This action forced many students who were enrolled in brick-and-mortar schools to begin learning virtually. As many brick-and-mortar schools had previously developed no infrastructure for virtual learning, there were challenges in effectively teaching the students in this manner, as was discovered by researcher Ian Kingsbury. Kingsbury[12] conducted a study of student and parent satisfaction with online learning experiences. He shared that while 86.4% of those interviewed: "agreed or strongly agreed" that children who had previously been enrolled in virtual schools when the pandemic started "learned a lot," just 13.4% of families of brick-and-mortar students, now learning virtually, agreed or strongly agreed that their children had learned "a lot" during the same time frame. Continuing, Kingsbury shared that the measure of differences in survey replies almost definitely proved that students enrolled in virtual schools learned more than did students enrolled in brick-and-mortar schools, as brick-and-mortar schools were attempting to function as virtual schools. To put it bluntly, many brick-and-mortar schools were caught flat-footed. The reason for this issue was found to be the compared training and preparation time of the two models. Virtual teachers were regularly trained and updated on virtual instruction, whereas brick-and-mortar teachers had, comparatively, little time to prepare for online teaching. Also, it is necessary to mention that virtual teachers were already doing the job and, through their "boots on the ground" regimen, were the default experts of the daily ins and outs of virtual learning simply from consistently working in this environment. Ultimately, Kingsbury found that students enrolled in virtual schools learned more in the virtual setting than did brick-and-mortar students learning in an environment that had been quickly adapted from brick-and-mortar to virtual. Emulating the brick-and-mortar classroom in a virtual setting created a truly unique set of challenges for both teachers and students. However, virtual schools did not face this issue, as the virtual model was built specifically for virtual learning in virtual environments. Yay us!

Given the fact that virtual K–12 schools had already been functioning, many for more than a decade, with competent experience and an infrastructure for virtual learning, it is not a surprise that the number of students enrolled in virtual schools spiked before and during the 2020–2021 school year, as many parents were concerned both about the COVID-19 pandemic and the challenges faced by brick-and-mortar schools in adapting to the pandemic. The quality of this particular online education model was in question.

In the United States, 9% of parents who had not homeschooled their children in the 2019–2020 school year shared that they planned to home school their children at least some of the time during the 2020–2021 school year.[13] In the 2019–2020 school year, 3% of American families were already homeschooling their children. The pandemic-related additions brought the number of virtual students to roughly 12% of all K–12 students for the 2020–2021 school year.[14] Nine percent of students indicates a major increase in overall virtual K–12 learners. In looking deeper into the data, the number of US K–12 students enrolled in school in 2019 was approximately 56.6 million.[15]

Roughly, this brings the number of American students who attended virtual school in the 2020–2021 school year to 6.6 million, up approximately 4.9 million from the 2019–2020 estimate of 1.7 million. Ultimately, the COVID-19 pandemic brought about unique circumstances, and schools adapted as they were able. However, virtual schools were built for online instruction. As a result, many people placed their trust, at least during the pandemic, in virtual schools.

Student Reasons for Choosing a Virtual Classroom

Personally, I have worked with students from many different backgrounds. From child stars in television shows and in movies to homeless students moving from place to place, and nearly every situation in-between, people choose virtual education for various reasons. Aside from the pandemic, families are drawn to virtual education for both personal and educational reasons. Regardless of how or why a student came to enroll in a virtual education environment, the teacher-student relationship is a vital piece of student success.

With regard to traditional teaching in the K–12 environment, a one-size-fits-all model has often been implemented in the US, with little concern given to individualized student needs and differences. However, the decision to differentiate instruction was unavoidable given the growing variance of student need in modern classrooms.[16] Families attend virtual schools due to problems with public schools, religion, increased one-to-one student to learning coach attention, and control over curriculum.[17] It is important to know why a family chose the virtual model, as it lends a glance into the family dynamic. Regardless of family reason for enrollment, the virtual teacher must plan for deliberate interaction with each student.

The Question of Interaction

A question that accompanies the growth of the population of virtual K–12 students is one of teacher-student interaction and the potential for building meaningful and productive teacher-student relationships in the virtual classroom environment. The issue of the significance of teacher-student interaction in this environment is important, as that connection could be the difference between student success or student failure.[18] Through this study, I attempted to better understand the ways in which virtual middle school teachers build those meaningful and productive relationships with their virtual middle school students.

Emulating the Brick-and-Mortar Classroom in the Virtual Environment

Simulating the brick-and-mortar classroom in a virtual setting has been found to be challenging. In looking at encouraging data on teaching in the virtual classroom, we have found that synchronous virtual classes can, at times, simulate the classroom environment, thus allowing students an experience vaguely similar to that of a live brick-and-mortar class.[19] However, instead of being held in-person, virtual courses take place utilizing a computer screen, while doing away with the physical presence of a teacher. Although virtual instructors find themselves in a position to teach live with their students, the idea of emulating brick-and-mortar classroom teaching may be unnatural and uncomfortable to some, as many teachers rely on physically seeing and working with students in an in-person setting to operate effectively.[20]

In discussing reasons for the difficulties of simulating the brick-and-mortar classroom in a virtual setting, we have found that introverted students may be likely to shy away from participating in class, when given the option of being silent in a virtual environment. The virtual environment grants students a much greater opportunity to "hide" from interaction than does the brick-and-mortar classroom, as the physical proximity of teachers to students is key to interaction. In the virtual environment, students often turn off their mics and cameras and, when asked a question by a teacher, reply that they are experiencing "tech issues." I have personally heard this reason for lack of participation hundreds of times. The idea of students hiding and, often getting lost, in the virtual environment is yet another reason that the virtual teacher must go above and beyond in building those ever-so-crucial teacher-student relationships.

Synchronous versus Asynchronous Virtual Teaching

Virtual teaching has been observed to be best when synchronous rather than asynchronous. To many instructors, synchronous teaching has been found to yield better results than has the creation of prerecorded video lectures that are never meant to be seen in a live classroom environment and that may or may not be viewed by students at all.[21] Similarly, methods for delivering virtual lectures asynchronously fail to reproduce the live teacher-student experience.[22]

When teachers in virtual classrooms avoid prepackaged, prerecorded lectures, and instead deliver their content live, inviting feedback and questions, as well as providing opportunities for student engagement, the virtual mode of teaching and lesson delivery can come close to resembling that of the brick-and-mortar classroom environment.[23] However, strictly virtual environments need not work to emulate a brick-and-mortar classroom. In my experience, most successful virtual classrooms embrace the virtual model, recognizing its own, distinctive merit, never attempting to replicate the brick-and-mortar setting. The idea that live lessons work better in delivering instruction to students than do asynchronous lessons is true regardless of classroom model and is an attribute of not only brick-and-mortar schools but also virtual schools.

Dissatisfaction Drives Change

For as long as there has been education, there have been ideas to improve the student experience. The US has seen the very idea of school shift over time as different approaches have been designed and implemented. Dissatisfaction with failing schools and with perceived complacency regarding traditional schools' approaches and educational delivery methods have combined to force policy changes.[24] These changes often involve the creation of, or growth of, new models of schools, including virtual schools. Again, this growth of virtual schools was on global display as a response to the failings of brick-and-mortar schools, as they attempted to emulate the brick-and-mortar setting, virtually, during the COVID-19 pandemic. While new models have come and gone and come again, the concept of teacher-student relationships is consistent as a key factor in student success, regardless of the setting.[25]

The participants in this study have taught both virtually and in brick-and-mortar classrooms, as have I. They have experienced the differences, some subtle and some obvious in the two models. So, how have they made the virtual model work for themselves and their students? It all begins with student engagement.

In September 2021, my wife, my two-year-old daughter, and my best friend, Steve, flew to Boston for my doctoral hooding ceremony. At the ceremony, one of the keynote speakers discussed the importance of the dissertation and of our research. This man challenged the graduates to not just allow our dissertations to sit unnoticed online. Rather, he stated, we should use our research to create and share a tool that could be useful to others. That is my hope for this book. I hope you learn a few useful tips and tricks along the way.

NOTES

1. Molnar, A., Miron, G., Elgeberi, N., Barbour, M. K., Huerta, L., Shafer, S. R., & Rice, J. K. (2019). Virtual schools in the U.S., 2019. National Education Policy Center. http://nepc.colorado.edu/publication/virtual-schools-annual-2019

2. Adkins, D., & Guerreiro, M. (2018). Learning styles: Considerations for technology enhanced item design. *British Journal of Educational Technology, 49*(3), 574–583.

3. Toppin, I. N., & Toppin, S. M. (2016). Virtual schools: The changing landscape of K–12 education in the U.S. *Education and Information Technologies, 21*(6), 1571–1581.

4. Mohd Khalid, M. N., & Quick, D. (2016). Teaching presence influencing online students' course satisfaction at an institution of higher education. *International Education Studies, 9*(3), 62–70.

5. Samuelsohn, D., Merisotis, J., Grunwald, M., Crow, M., Dabars, W., & Remondi, J. (2015, September 23). Virtual schools are booming. Who's paying attention? *Politico.* www.politico.com/agenda/story/2015/09/virtual-schools-education-000227

6. Molnar, A., Miron, G., Elgeberi, N., Barbour, M. K., Huerta, L., Shafer, S. R., & Rice, J. K. (2019). Virtual schools in the U.S. 2019. National Education Policy Center. http://nepc.colorado.edu/publication/virtual-schools-annual-2019

7. K12 Inc. (2021). *School Mission.* https://www.k12.com/about-k12/company-mission.html

8. EducationData.org. (2020). *K–12 School Enrollment & Student Population Statistics.* https://educationdata.org/k12-enrollment-statistics

9. EducationData.org. (2020). *K–12 School Enrollment & Student Population Statistics.* https://educationdata.org/k12-enrollment-statistics

10. K12 Inc. (2022). *Over 1 million students have chosen public school at home with K12!* https://www.k12.com/about-k12/million-students.html. Kaufmann, R., Sellnow, D. D., & Frisby, B. N. (2015). The development and validation of the online learning climate scale (OLCS). *Communication Education, 65*(3), 307–321.

11. Strauss, V. (2020, March 27). 1.5 billion children around globe affected by school closure: What countries are doing to keep kids learning during pandemic. *The Washington Post.* www.washingtonpost.com/education/2020/03/26/nearly-14-billion-children-around-globe-are-out-school-heres-what-countries-are-doing-keep-kids-learning-during-pandemic/

12. Kingsbury, I. (2020). *Online learning: How do brick and mortar schools stack up to virtual schools?* EdChoice. https://www.edchoice.org/wp-content/uploads/2020/09/09-20-Virtual-Schools-During-COVID-UPDATED-1.pdf

13. Prothero, A., & Samuels, C. A. (2021, February 25). Home schooling is way up with COVID-19. Will it last? *Education Week.* www.edweek.org/policy-politics/home-schooling-is-way-up-with-covid-19-will-it-last/2020/11

14. Prothero, A., & Samuels, C. A. (2021, February 25). Home schooling is way up with COVID-19. Will it last? *Education Week.* www.edweek.org/policy-politics/home-schooling-is-way-up-with-covid-19-will-it-last/2020/11

15. EducationData.org. (2020). *K–12 School Enrollment & Student Population Statistics.* https://educationdata.org/k12-enrollment-statistics

16. Subban, P. (2006). A research basis supporting differentiated instruction. *International Education Journal, 7*(7), 935–947.

17. Dowshen, S. (2015). Homeschooling (for kids). The Nemours Foundation. www.kidshealth.org/en/kids/homeschool.html#:~:text=Parents%20choose%20to%20homeschool%20their,than%20the%20local%20school%20can

18. Samuelsohn, D., Merisotis, J., Grunwald, M., Crow, M., Dabars, W., & Remondi, J. (2015, September 23). Virtual schools are booming. Who's paying attention? *Politico.* www.politico.com/agenda/story/2015/09/virtual-schools-education-000227

19. Estelami, H. (2017). The pedagogical and institutional impact of disruptive innovations in distance business education. *American Journal of Business Education, 10*(3), 97–108.

20. Subban, P. (2006). A research basis supporting differentiated instruction. *International Education Journal, 7*(7), 935–947.

21. Subban, P. (2006). A research basis supporting differentiated instruction. *International Education Journal, 7*(7), 935–947.

22. Ke, F., & Chavez, A. F. (2013). *Web-based teaching and learning across culture and age.* Springer.

23. Laborie, K., & Stone, T. (2015). *Interact and engage! 50+ activities for virtual training, meetings and webinars.* Association for Talent Development.

24. Samuelsohn, D., Merisotis, J., Grunwald, M., Crow, M., Dabars, W., & Remondi, J. (2015, September 23). Virtual schools are booming. Who's paying attention? *Politico.* www.politico.com/agenda/story/2015/09/virtual-schools-education-000227

25. Mohd Khalid, M. N., & Quick, D. (2016). Teaching presence influencing online students' course satisfaction at an institution of higher education. *International Education Studies, 9*(3), 62–70.

Chapter 1

Participants

This chapter will introduce the reader to the participants in this study. Each participant was interviewed, using internet technology such as Zoom and Newrow. Again, names have been changed to protect anonymity.

DAISY

Daisy identifies as Caucasian and prefers the pronouns she, her, and hers. She was born in Florida but grew up in Ojai, California. She attended elementary and high school in Summerland, and Ojai, California. Her undergraduate degree is in health science, and she has a master's degree in education. Her original plan was to become a physical therapist, but she later switched to focus on education. She has never been a virtual student at any level of school. When asked to discuss the first time she heard about virtual schooling, she stated:

> I actually heard of it, well, when I was pregnant with my daughter. How did I hear about it? There was Fig Springs School in Ojai, and that was the first distance learning school that I had learned about. I tried to get a job there and the lady found out I was pregnant and didn't give me a job. . . . There was another one that I looked into as well.
>
> Then I just started researching different virtual opportunities, just so I could stay home with my child. I stumbled upon the Violetta Virtual Academy. It was just basically through research. So that's how it all got started.

TAMMY

Tammy identifies as Caucasian and prefers the pronouns she, her, and hers. Tammy is originally from Boston, Massachusetts, and came to California later in life. She has been a virtual student during her master's degree program and in the completion of her teaching credential program. Tammy considers herself to be a "big advocate" of virtual education. Tammy's answers were the shortest of all the participants. She gave no-nonsense, to-the-point responses to the research questions. When prompted, she gave little in the way of storytelling. Still, her answers to the research questions were observed and analyzed.

BOBBI

Bobbi also identifies as Caucasian and prefers the pronouns she, her, and hers. Bobbi grew up in several different locations. She described her upbringing in this way:

> I went to a K–8 school in Pennsylvania for kindergarten, first, second, and I think part of third. That was the longest I was ever at one school. Then, we moved to Chicago where the schools were amazing. It was a really nice suburb of Chicago, and the school system was amazing. I did fourth grade there and fifth grade there, and then we moved to Germany. And then, I went to German school for one year, which was really, really crazy.
>
> My brother is two years younger, was two grades behind me, and we both started in the same kindergarten class and basically you went to kindergarten until you could learn that and then you would go to first grade until you could learn that, but we lost a lot of education, as you can imagine, because we didn't speak any German. I would come home from school and watch *Sesamstrasse*, which was Sesame Street, and *Schtroumpf*, which was the Smurfs, because I knew them in English, and I was trying to teach myself quick German. That was a really interesting experience because I essentially was a GSL student. I get how English-language learners feel. It was hard.
>
> I would come home; I would be so tired after school from trying to learn stuff that I would come home and go to bed. Come home and take a nap for an hour and then try to do my homework. I just remember being super tired from trying to learn everything. We did that for a year, and then my parents put us in the Department of Defense school, the regular American school.
>
> My dad was not in the military, so for us it was like a private school. We had to pay to go, but for the kids who were in the military and the Embassy, they could go for free. That was a little bit better. I still took German, but it was an American school, so math was in English and whatever was in English.

Bobbi stated that she has lived in several different locations as an adult, as well.

> I've been in California now for six years . . . and I really never want to leave. Before California, we were in Pennsylvania, and before Pennsylvania, we were

in Massachusetts, and before that, we were in New Jersey, and before that we were in Maryland. I went to college in Virginia, and then I also lived in Canada and in Germany.

Bobbi's varied experiences have shaped her views on education, as well as having a specific impact on her outlook on the struggles facing students for whom English is a second language.

In terms of being a virtual student, Bobbi stated that her master's program at the University of Southern California (USC) had been virtual. She found the virtual program to be "phenomenal." Bobbie credits peer work with students utilizing web cameras for her positive master's experience. In connecting her experience to her occupational aspirations, Bobbi stated:

> To be honest with you, it was so great that that's when I'm like: "I do believe in virtual education," and I went off and actively sought a job teaching online for that reason. I felt like it was the wave of the future.

Bobbi's vast experience with education led her to seek out VIVA.

> I was like: "I wonder if this exists for a K–8 group," and sure enough, found VIVA, got an interview, got the job. I felt like it was fate. I really did.

JILL

Jill identifies as Hispanic and prefers the pronouns she, her, and hers. She grew up in the central coast of California, near Santa Maria, where she attended public schools. Jill stated that she was always a good student.

> I was the kid who in kindergarten, came home and did their homework right away. I really liked the learning process. I excelled early in my education.

Jill struggled with dysfunction in her family, which might have made it difficult to focus all her attention on her studies, but she persevered. Not only did Jill succeed in school, but she also took time to work in the community. She shared:

> I did a lot of things with community service and sport and things like writing on the school paper and things like that. I did really well throughout. And then I actually ended up graduating early and took my AP credits in college early, just because I was forced to move out of my house.

Like the other participants, Jill's experience with virtual schooling was solely in college. At Chapman University, her undergraduate program of study was a political science and history double major. She then earned teaching credentials in mild and moderate disability for special education, as well as her multiple-subject credentials and her single-subject credential in social science. Of her time as a virtual student, Jill shared that her experience was: "amazing." She shared:

> You'd be in a lecture hall with this amazing, visiting professor. But then I could take it online because I would just be in the class at the library or whatever, or sometimes they would do like satellite conferences. You go to class, but then you have virtual elements. I know that's standard practice now, but that was the emerging thing when I started college, and it was really beneficial because it provided a lot more access to my professors.

Jill shared that her positive experiences as a virtual student led to her seeking out employment as a virtual teacher.

JOY

Joy identifies as Caucasian and prefers the pronouns she, her, and hers. She grew up in southern California, in the Inland Empire. Joy's story of her educational journey was told as such.

> As a student, I went to private school on scholarships. I was always the really poor kid that people took pity on, so I had lots of scholarships which was really beneficial, and I didn't realize it at the time, and I kind of squandered a lot of the opportunities that I had because I didn't do the extra work. So, I really empathize with my students who have the ability but don't have the motivation, I think.
>
> And my mom was a single mom, and she worked all the time, so I really can relate to some of our students that are kind of floating out there on their own. . . . And then I was sent off to college after school in Oregon. I was kind of a troubled teen, and so I was given the choice to go to this college that I got another scholarship for from our church, and the caveat was that they would pay for everything as long as I stayed . . . it was like a bible college. I was expelled rather quickly and sent home for reasons I won't get into, and then I came home, met a boy, moved in with a boy, started working, and then realized: "Oh, I kind of need an education," and it was exactly what I needed because then it was my problem, and it wasn't anybody else's problem.
>
> So, I went to night school. Took me about seven years. Got my business degree and started working in accounting. Lost my job the last big recession

and went back to school nights to get my teaching credential, and here I am 10, 11 years later.

In detailing her experience as a virtual student, Joy shared:

> I did virtual classes for college, so I took a couple of online classes when that was brand-new in community college, and at some point, during my credential, I took an online class to get the constitution done or something. . . . I really liked it because I felt like it gave me anonymity in a certain sense, which bred a little bit of confidence. And I wasn't worried about what people thought of my appearance or in my awkward pauses or when I start to stutter because you could really type out a lot of your answers, and that made me feel a little more confident because I'm better with typing than speaking.

Joy shared that her experience as a virtual student coincided with enrolling her own children into VIVA. Thus, Joy was a VIVA parent before she was a VIVA teacher.

KAREN

Karen identifies as white, with Irish and Welsh heritage. She prefers the pronouns she, her, and hers. Karen grew up in Culver City, California, which is where she resides today. She stated that she attended public school in Culver City Unified School District, sharing that she always enjoyed school. Karen was happy to tell her story. She shared:

> I always had a pretty positive outlook on school, was always a pretty decent student, very much looked forward to going to school every day. I enjoyed pretty much everything that school had to offer, the academic part, the social part, and even the after-school part too. . . . So, college, I did junior colleges first.
> I went to Santa Monica Junior College first. . . . I ended up going to West LA after that, because it was much closer, and the programs were much less impacted than at Santa Monica College. . . . So, I was the second graduating class from UC Merced. It was a brand-new school when I went there, but brand-new facilities, we had excellent professors there. . . . by 2008 I had started a program with USC to get my masters and my teaching credential. So that's kind of where my real teaching career began . . . it turned out that USC had a brand-new program where you'd be going to school online, and you'd do your field work at the schools of your choice in your community. So, that really appealed to me because I could still work part time [and] go to school. . . .
> The last school that I attended to clear my credential was also an online program and that was through San Diego State University . . . the master's program

with USC was the first purely virtual program [I attended]. Or not purely, but primarily online program that I did.

Before that in junior college there were a couple of classes that I had taken as online courses, so that in junior college that would have been the first time that I had any idea of what an online education looks like. . . . the USC program was kind of a hybrid online and then in person for the student teaching part. And then the clear credential program was SDSU, that was purely online. . . .

When discussing what she liked about the virtual programs she attended, Karen shared:

I always enjoyed being a virtual student. I'm kind of like a shy, awkward person when I'm in person. So, I felt like I could kind of be more myself when I was online and communicating with teachers and that part of it. I also really enjoy the saving of time, like I don't have go show up and meet up in person at a certain time and place. So, I like that flexibility and I like the saving of time from not having to commute to different places. So, that's really what appealed to me initially.

I did realize though that it does take quite a bit of like. . . . I don't want to say independence, but the ability to kind of set your own schedule and stick by it, and that's something that I had struggled with before. So, I did have to teach myself how to stay strict on that. I think my first couple of online classes that I took were kind of disasters because I would wait until a huge deadline to get a bunch of things done, and that's not really the case with every online program. You can really do that. So, I had to teach myself that in the first couple of online courses that I ever took, that that's not really the way to go. So, it took a little bit of time to get used to that.

Karen shared that she had always felt like a teacher. She had an uncle who taught school and thought that teaching could be a good fit for her. She also explained how her own experience as a virtual student attracted her to the idea of becoming a virtual teacher.

It seemed like a cool idea, because I had done so much of my own education as an online student. I thought it would be an interesting challenge to take on the online teacher role. I didn't think that I'd like it as much as I do. I thought that it would be something that I'd spend a couple of years doing and then move on.

But I like the unique challenges that online teaching brings, and I think that online teaching is pretty important for certain populations of our students. Definitely not all, because I think it takes a special kind of person to be a teacher for online teaching, and it takes a special kind of student to be successful in an online school. So, there's definitely a huge need for it, for the right student population. And then there's definitely also teachers that either love it or hate it, and I'm one of the ones that happens to love it.

MICHELLE

Michelle identifies as Caucasian and prefers the pronouns she, her, and hers. She grew up in the Bay Area of California. Michelle's educational story is one of low self-esteem that was boosted through acceptance and care from good teachers. She shared:

> Elementary school I changed pretty often. Changed schools pretty often, just because we moved. Trying to make friends was always kind of hard. I was very introverted, so it took some skills, but it went okay. Most of my teachers, overall, they were pretty great. Middle school was in private school, which was brand-new. My whole sixth grade, through eighth grade classes were like twenty-five-ish kids, so we were all one tight-knit group. That's really all we knew. I moved in the middle of eighth grade, so I had to go to a different school . . . which was a bigger school from what I knew. . . . High school was something else.
>
> I was always kind of the outsider of the class. I hung out with whoever decided that they were going to like me. Overall, the teachers were pretty good. Geometry was kind of my biggest one. That teacher, she has a reputation of being really bad and not really caring. My experiences were kind of proof of that. I know that failing that class was because I couldn't understand the topic, and every time I went for help it didn't help. She really didn't help. It always gave me the impression that I was annoying her because I'd asked a question. Which then, my junior year taking algebra two and trying to take geometry online by myself, that didn't work out well.
>
> Most of my other classes were good. I liked the teachers. Got along pretty well. Senior year I found out if I don't pass geometry I will not graduate, so I ended up having to give up this class I really liked, which was kind of like the internship that they offered. I worked in the geometry book with a different teacher. Her name was Ms. Nakamori. She's probably one of my favorite teachers, just because she actually cared. She taught me the way I got it. I ended up passing that with a B and graduating high school. That was huge. . . . College I did junior college for about three years to figure out what I wanted to do. Once a day I went to a tutor and graduated there in 2013. Got my teaching credential the year later.

Michelle is living proof that a meaningful and productive teacher-student relationship can make all the difference. Her experience as a virtual student took place in high school when she was made to redo geometry. Of her virtual experience, Michelle shared:

> It was okay. I was kind of left on my own to do it. They have the modules. They have the practice stuff. To pass this class I had to take a final, and if I didn't pass

the first time, I had to take it a second time. I ended up not passing it that way, but the program was set up nice. It just didn't really work for me.

Although Michelle did not enjoy her personal experience as a virtual student, she sought out virtual teaching in hopes of helping students who had been marginalized for one reason or another. She hoped to be the Ms. Nakamori to those students.

MIKE

Mike identifies as Mexican American/Hispanic/Latino. He shared that he is: "really not sure on classification of that. It's changed over the years." He prefers the pronouns he, him, and his. Mike grew up in Oxnard, California, and currently resides in nearby Ventura, California. In sharing his educational story, Mike stated:

> As a young student, so elementary, I was flagged for a GATE, gifted and talented education, program when I was in first grade for math. I stayed in the program up until I was in eighth grade. We shipped around quite a bit, so the program moved, so I was bused at a distance from whatever my local school was. When I got in high school, I wasn't really that interested in school as much anymore, so I didn't really focus on it. It wasn't really until college that I found what I liked or what worked for me.

Mike shared that his only experience as a virtual student was in completing his teaching credential. He described his experience as such:

> It was good. It was different. It fell in line with what I needed at the time. I believe when I started my teaching program, my daughter was probably about five, give or take. Five or six, something like that. We were in the middle of the economic downturn in 2010, 2012. Just being able to go to school at home actually made a huge, huge difference. Then I did need to go into school and do student teaching, I think once or twice a week.

Mike shared that carrying over his experience from days of working in a brick-and-mortar school has helped him in addressing student needs in the virtual environment.

Each of the participants in this study comes from a background that is unique and specific. However, all were drawn to virtual K–8 learning. Through their experiences, each teacher has developed methods, tips, and tricks that nurture success in the virtual environment. Throughout my discussions with these teachers, common threads emerged, as each educator unknowingly overlapped big ideas regarding the building of productive and meaningful teacher-student relationships in virtual environments with those of their colleagues. It is my hope that this collective wisdom will help you, the reader, as you plan for managing your virtual classroom.

Chapter 2

Student Engagement

Obviously, by now, student engagement has been found to be a crucial factor in student success, regardless of educational model. Engagement is substantial in its influence on student satisfaction and success in virtual learning environments.[1] Students who engage in their courses often experience more satisfaction and, in turn, perform better academically than students who are disengaged.[2]

A few key aspects in the fostering of student engagement are the perception of teacher social presence in the course, student academic involvement, and the establishment of a supportive educational environment.[3] It is not just any interaction that matters. Rather, the social teacher-student interaction and the student's perception of a teacher's social presence are each crucial to the enhancement of student engagement.

When looking at the issue of teacher-student relationships in virtual settings, one significant aspect of consideration is student and family satisfaction or dissatisfaction regarding the quality and style of educational delivery. Rates of satisfaction often correlate positively with student success rates.[4] Data from a few studies has found that the dominant determinant of student satisfaction is often teaching presence.[5]

Teaching presence, when incorporated positively, has demonstrated direct and indirect effects on student satisfaction. Further, in putting the pieces together, a correlation has been discovered among teaching presence, student satisfaction, and student achievement.[6] Research and personal experience have each taught me that when teachers are consistently, socially, and academically present, virtual students will be, generally, content with their coursework, thus creating a setting that is both satisfactory and conducive to student academic achievement.

DEFINING STUDENT ENGAGEMENT

Although *student engagement* is a term that is common in any educational setting, defining student engagement is not a simple task. In fact, there is disagreement about what goes into the idea of student engagement. To be sure there is no evident definition of student engagement.[7] This absence of definition makes the act of measuring engagement a difficult one. Student engagement, then, is a multifaceted construct.

One point of agreement in the literature is the idea that any definition of student engagement would need to include three key elements. To adequately define student engagement, behavioral, cognitive, and emotional engagement each need to be considered.[8] Behavioral engagement can be broken down into segments, including attendance, participation, following classroom rules, and etiquette, while at the same time meeting teacher and institutional expectations.[9]

Cognitive engagement typically signifies the personal investment each student makes in their own learning, such as understanding and making an effort to understand complex ideas. This type of engagement is often described as being meaningful and focused. Cognitively engaged students tend to regulate their own learning by preparing, checking, and regularly assessing their progress.[10] Emotional engagement is identified through teacher and student recognition of constructive student responses regarding the classroom setting. This engagement involves student constructive engagement with the teachers, other students, the curriculum, and the school itself. It also includes the student's relationship with their own academic progress.[11] Research has uncovered the idea that these three strands of student engagement are interdependent, as students should be behaviorally and emotionally involved in classroom tasks, feeling both relaxed and connected, before they are able to become cognitively engaged.[12] These considerations fit within Garrison, Anderson, and Archer's community of inquiry model, which utilizes social presence, cognitive presence, and teaching presence.[13]

Given this deconstruction, the complex construct that is student engagement becomes more understandable. Teacher-student relationships benefit when teachers are able to define, better understand, and work with the individual pieces of student engagement. This cognizance of the pieces of the whole allows for better teacher preparation regarding opportunities for engagement.

When effective, teacher presence often leads to consistent and rich student engagement. Without student engagement, lesson plans are meaningless. Students must be engaged in course content if the construction of working knowledge is to be the result.[14] Similarly, when student academic engagement is high and when students view school as valuable, while exhibiting proactive academic participation, academic success is a likely outcome.[15] Hence, student engagement is often the deciding factor in student success. However, that engagement is typically the result of a teacher's plans for opportunities for student interaction with the teacher, the curriculum, and with other students. When the teacher recognizes the needs of the specific classroom in question, student opportunities for engagement must be considered.

Although the stimulation of student engagement in any class setting may be challenging, student engagement in virtual environments can be especially difficult to cultivate. Engagement in a virtual classroom can be distant and detached when compared to student engagement in brick-and-mortar settings, as students in brick-and-mortar settings are able to interact in person with teachers, whereas virtual students interact with teachers through live and asynchronous video classes, discussion boards, emails, video calls, and other educational software. When compared, the connection between teacher and student is vastly different depending on the educational model and needs to be treated as such.

NURTURING STUDENT ENGAGEMENT

A considerable piece of the equation when observing teacher-student relationships in virtual environments is the given methodology chosen by the teacher to nurture student engagement and student interaction with the teacher. Academically, the act of a teacher asking direct questions is central to the facilitation of student engagement. Direct questions and prompts from the teacher can be a strong predictor of enhanced interactivity.[16] Similarly, student engagement increases when instructors personalize instruction, as well as engage in social interactions with students.

Again, we see social interactions mentioned as a crucial factor in student success. This personalization ultimately leads to the building of meaningful and productive teacher-student relationships, while nurturing student academic success. A common and plausible conclusion to be drawn here is the notion that deliberate teacher action holds real influence over student academic engagement. Clearly, instructor interactivity with students is vital to the fostering of student engagement in the virtual classroom. Ultimately, whether the classroom is virtual or brick-and-mortar, meaningful and deliberate teacher facilitation of opportunities for engagement is vital to student engagement.

Although always significant, student engagement becomes an especially crucial piece of the learning process as students proceed from elementary to middle school, as this age sees a marked decrease in enthusiasm. This decline is observed academically, as well as in terms of confidence and student-student and teacher-student relationships. Further, it has been found that student engagement suffers during and after the transition from K–5 to middle school.[17] Estimations are found to be in the ballpark of 40% of students who show signs of disengagement as they begin middle school.[18] This disengagement can manifest as indifference, lack of academic drive, or as decreased attention span.[19]

Further, researchers have found that a great deal of student lapse in terms of enthusiasm is directly linked to teaching methods and classroom models that do not meet the developmental requirements of the students. Thus, a detachment of teaching methods from student needs can both decrease student engagement and produce substandard academic results. This detachment also hinders the formation of meaningful and productive teacher-student relationships.

STUDENT AUTONOMY

There is a delicate balance that teeters between student success and student failure when granting students autonomy in a virtual educational setting. It is true that autonomy may foster independent work. However, too much independence may create an environment in which a teacher loses their own engagement in class activities, leading to lowered student engagement.

Granting students ownership over educational and behavioral aspects of a given classroom, often reserved for authority figures, has long been a known and successful teaching method utilized to invite student buy-in on classroom rules and policies. Similarly, the granting of some autonomy can be a motivation for student success. However, this autonomy must be approached with careful planning. Self-directed motivation, which can result from the teacher's facilitation of opportunities for students to take the lead on decision-making, can lead to heightened student engagement.[20] It has been my experience that student engagement increases when a teacher is responsive to student input. Conversely, student engagement has been found to regress when teachers do not respect or acknowledge the value of student input.[21]

In terms of student success, students in an environment that stressed peer review over the traditional teacher-student model and students with more autonomy tended to see better academic success than did those in a traditional classroom setting.[22] Findings such as these give credibility to the idea that the teacher-student relationship is at its strongest when students are trusted with a degree of autonomy; however, that degree will vary from student to student.

Overall, too much autonomy has been found to be detrimental to student engagement. Again, tying teacher presence to student engagement, we find that reduced student engagement is often a product of a lack of teacher engagement in classroom learning activities. Teachers, including myself and those who participated in this study, have recognized that their own engagement did, in fact, affect student engagement.

Teachers have found that if they were not sufficiently focused on the facilitation of student learning, such as prompting students to take part in classroom discussions while inspiring and encouraging them, student engagement tended to regress. Similarly, teachers in Louwrens's and Hartnett's 2015 study shared that it was essential for them to remain focused on a given project or assignment and to make sure interactions with students offered useful direction, encouragement, and reassurance.[23] Further, a lack of validation from teachers to students has been known to create a regression in student engagement and enthusiasm.

Going a step further, reasonable but stern discipline in the classroom when coupled with encouraging teacher-student interactions was found to be positively correlated with greater student academic engagement and higher grades while also inspiring student-directed goals.[24] Schools that coupled discipline with student support have been found to create high levels of student engagement. Discipline in a virtual setting often relies on the student-parent-teacher dynamic, as well as the noncompliance protocols of the school in question.

Regarding autonomy in general, some students are simply not equipped to be independent learners.[25] One aspect of this discovery on considering autonomous student engagement came from Avery, Huggan, and Preston,[26] who stated that a lack of critical thinking skills in young students could be problematic. Continuing, they shared that many students are used to being given the answers and often need immediate feedback to know whether their answers are correct.

Too much autonomy does not allow for this kind of immediate feedback. Thus, in some situations, especially in virtual environments, autonomy has been shown to hinder student academic success. Ultimately, the amount of autonomy given by a teacher to a virtual student comes down to the teacher-student relationship and what is deemed practical and productive, given each individual situation.

STUDENT FEELINGS AND ATTITUDES

When discussing student autonomy and engagement, it is important to consider student feelings and attitudes. Teenage students are often focused on the need for a permissive view of their chosen actions, as they understand that school is typically rigid with prearranged expectations and rules.[27] Adolescent students are, thus, greatly interested in the ways in which teachers and other educational stakeholders willingly work with them as they navigate the challenges of middle school.[28]

The promotion of student independence partially hinges on the teacher's willingness to invite students to utilize their own creativity and problem-solving skills to complete tasks rather than providing students a rigid one-size-fits-all technique.[29] The act of giving students greater autonomy in their educational tasks has been found to further inspire students to connect to their educational endeavors, as well as generating a greater interest in the content, due to the feeling of personal meaningfulness found in a given process.[30] Thus, a substantial piece of the equation is the notion that even when students are granted a degree of autonomy, student engagement depends on active interaction from a teacher, as well as the balance that is struck between teacher-facilitated and student-directed activities.

Autonomy is quite different in a virtual setting than it is in a brick-and-mortar environment, as students are more prone to feeling alone and isolated in a virtual setting as they experience what is, to them, a void in peer comradery. Thus, teacher-student relationships rely on the balance between teacher-directed activities and a given amount of student autonomy. There is no perfect formula for this mixture, as each situation is different, but regardless of the environment, a teacher needs to be mindful of the ways in which autonomy is influencing student engagement and the teacher-student relationship. Teachers in virtual environments need to be especially aware of the effects of student autonomy on student academic success, as a lack of direct teacher input may leave students feeling alone and could lead to an overall lack of student engagement.

RESULTS OF STUDENT ENGAGEMENT ON ACADEMIC ACHIEVEMENT

It seems obvious that students with high academic engagement tend to succeed academically more so than those who are not as immersed. Fittingly, the literature on academic engagement supports this hypothesis, aligning a lack of student engagement with lowered academic results. One of the realities regarding lack of student engagement is the fact that students who are actively engaged in school are simply less likely to drop out of school.[31] When working with middle school students, it is important to be cognizant that the idea of dropping out of school begins earlier than high school, as it has been discovered that the academic performance of middle schoolers and their academic engagement have been key forecasters of high school graduation and dropout rates.[32]

Students who show a respect for their education and understand its importance and implications for the future are more likely to succeed academically, graduating at higher rates than students who do not.[33] Outcomes regarding the cause-and-effect relationship between student academic engagement and academic success, as well as dropout rates, have been found to be directly related to student detachment from education, well before high school.[34] Again, this detachment has been found to develop in middle school.

Many students considered to be susceptible to dropping out of school were found to be disconnected from their education before ever beginning high school. As a solution to this problem, many "inventive" high school models and programs have recently arisen. The problem with this approach, however, lies with the idea that regardless of how inventive a high school program is, and can be to student engagement and success, many students begin leaving school, or thinking about leaving school, before ever giving inventive high school programs a chance to take hold or giving them an opportunity to change their minds.[35] Further, it has been found that student behavioral and psychosocial engagement tends to deteriorate quickly during the middle school years.[36] Disengaged students reach high school with little confidence as to the value of education.

The onus is, once again, on the middle school teacher to prevent disengagement early on in each student's academic experience, especially when that experience takes place in a virtual environment. Catching a lack of engagement early can be the difference between a high school graduate and a high school dropout. No pressure!

The literature clearly states that student engagement is directly connected to academic outcome. This connection underscores the importance of virtual teachers building meaningful and productive relationships with their students, as students who feel supported are often more engaged and productive than students who do not feel as supported. In a virtual setting, students may feel isolated and disconnected from teachers, peers, and curriculum. Thus, it is up to the virtual educator to bridge that gap, allowing for opportunities for student engagement and, ultimately, academic success.

THOUGHTS ON STUDENT ENGAGEMENT

Student engagement is a multifaceted concept that becomes even more complex when placed in the setting of the virtual classroom. The transactional distance between teacher and student is greater in this environment than in a brick-and-mortar school. Thus, the challenging task of ensuring student engagement falls squarely on the teacher. The obvious goal, given the research, has to be the building of meaningful and productive teacher-student relationships in the virtual classroom setting, as it has been found that teachers and students view these relationships as essential to the success of the virtual student.

By deliberately planning activities aimed at the development of teacher and student social presence, as well as student sense of belonging, the teachers were able to develop safe and productive virtual classrooms. Student engagement, when stressed in the early years, can lead to the nurturing of high school graduates rather than students who choose to drop out. Again, I must state that of the students considered to be susceptible to dropping out of high school, a great many initially became disengaged in middle school. These students mentally begin dropping out of high school before ever attending high school.[37] This is the danger of early disengagement.

Although important to learning and engagement, student autonomy has been found to be a challenging balance, as its granting causes some students to embrace the independence, while leaving others to feel abandoned, craving more teacher-led activities. Autonomy can be an effective tool utilized by teachers to enhance student engagement. However, when students are granted a degree of autonomy, student engagement ultimately depends on active interaction from a teacher and the balance that is struck between teacher-facilitated and student-directed activities.

Ultimately, student engagement leads to academic success. Regardless of the learning environment, it is the teacher who is charged with the facilitation of student engagement. Meaningful and productive teacher-student relationships are crucial to the cultivation of student engagement. The nurturing of student engagement has been found to be more difficult in a virtual classroom, as the transactional distance is greater in this environment than in a brick-and-mortar setting.

Reaching out to a student's family is central to bridging the gap that exists in the virtual classroom environment. The identification of a supportive educational community is necessary if meaningful and productive teacher-student relationships are to develop. Ultimately, for a student to become meaningfully engaged academically, a trusting and respectful teacher-student relationship must be developed. When a productive teacher-student relationship develops, student engagement increases.

Much like the special attention paid to teacher presence, a great deal of the challenging task of ensuring student engagement is, ultimately, the responsibility of the teacher, as the support that comes with building meaningful and productive teacher-student relationships is seen as crucial by both teachers and students when connecting in the virtual classroom environment. Student engagement, when stressed in the early years, can lead to the nurturing of students who are less likely to drop out of school.[38]

The vulnerability of many students who are most likely to drop out of school and the idea that these students tend to leave school early, especially when the student has become disengaged from education before high school, can be combatted by each teacher's decision to plan for enhanced student engagement in the virtual classroom. The danger of early disengagement is real. Student engagement is never guaranteed; thus, the opportunities for and encouragement of engagement are largely the responsibility of the teacher.

The teacher-student relationship becomes stronger and more productive when the teacher facilitates opportunities for meaningful student engagement. Gauging the amount of autonomy to entrust in students is a challenging balance, as its granting causes some students to embrace independence and blossom, while leaving others to feel neglected and desirous of more teacher-led activities.

Autonomy may be utilized in an effective manner when teachers wield it to improve student academic engagement. Nevertheless, when students are granted autonomy, student engagement still depends on active interaction from a teacher and the balance that is struck between teacher-facilitated and student-directed activities. Thus, teacher presence is deeply interwoven with student engagement in the establishment of meaningful and productive teacher-student relationships.

As with teacher presence, it is the teacher who is tasked with the facilitation of student engagement. Student engagement is imperative to academic success and to the establishment of meaningful and productive teacher-student relationships. The cultivation of student engagement has been found to be more difficult in the virtual environment than it is in the brick-and-mortar classroom, as the transactional distance is greater in the virtual environment.

Student recognition of an encouraging teacher and educational community of inquiry is compulsory for the building of meaningful and productive teacher-student relationships.[39] Ultimately, for a student to become academically engaged in a meaningful way, it is essential that a trusting and respectful teacher-student relationship be developed. When a productive teacher-student relationship develops, student engagement increases. Thus, it becomes clear that teacher presence and student engagement are intertwined concepts that when encouraged to grow help to solidify the teacher-student relationship and, ultimately, lead to student success.

As student engagement is ultimately necessary for the building of meaningful and productive teacher-student relationships and student success, it is threaded throughout each strand of teacher discussion that will follow in this book. It was simply impossible to separate student engagement from the other big ideas. Thus, discussion on student engagement may be found in the teacher conversations on transactional distance, teacher presence, students' sense of belonging, and community. The concept of student engagement is ubiquitous in the discussion regarding overall student success.

NOTES

1. Bitzer, P., & Janson, A. (2014). Towards a holistic understanding of technology mediated learning services: A state-of-the-art analysis. In: European Conference on Information Systems (ECIS). https://ssrn.com/abstract=2470946 *Proceedings of the European Conference on Information Systems,* 1–20.

2. Meyer, K. A. (2014). J-B ASHE higher education report series (AEHE): Student Engagement Online: What Works and Why. *ASHE Higher Education Report, 40*(6), 1–15. Jossey-Bass.

3. Hoskins, B. J. (2012). Connections, engagement, and presence. *Journal of Continuing Higher Education, 60*(1), 51–53.

4. Kucuk, S., & Richardson, J. C. (2019). A structural equation model of predictors of online learners' engagement and satisfaction. *Online Learning, 23*(2), 196–216.

5. Kucuk, S., & Richardson, J. C. (2019). A structural equation model of predictors of online learners' engagement and satisfaction. *Online Learning, 23*(2), 196–216.

6. Kucuk, S., & Richardson, J. C. (2019). A structural equation model of predictors of online learners' engagement and satisfaction. *Online Learning, 23*(2), 196–216.

7. Louwrens, N., & Hartnett, M. (2015). Student and teacher perceptions of online student engagement in an online middle school. *Journal of Open, Flexible and Distance Learning, 19*(1), 27–44.

8. Fredricks, J. A., Blumenfeld, P. C., & Paris, A. H. (2004). School engagement: Potential of the concept, state of the evidence. *Review of Educational Research, 74*(1), 59–109.

9. Fredricks, J. A., Blumenfeld, P. C., & Paris, A. H. (2004). School engagement: Potential of the concept, state of the evidence. *Review of Educational Research, 74*(1), 59–109.

10. Louwrens, N., & Hartnett, M. (2015). Student and teacher perceptions of online student engagement in an online middle school. *Journal of Open, Flexible and Distance Learning, 19*(1), 27–44.

11. Louwrens, N., & Hartnett, M. (2015). Student and teacher perceptions of online student engagement in an online middle school. *Journal of Open, Flexible and Distance Learning, 19*(1), 27–44.

12. Harris, L. R. (2008). A phenomenographic investigation of teacher conceptions of student engagement in learning. *The Australian Educational Researcher, 35*(1), 57–79.

13. Garrison, D. R., Anderson, T., & Archer, W. (1999). Critical inquiry in a text-based environment: Computer conferencing in higher education. *The Internet and Higher Education, 2*(2), 87–105.

14. Della Noce, D. J., Scheffel, D. L., & Lowry, M. (2014). Questions that get answered: The construction of instruction conversations on online asynchronous discussion boards. *Journal of Online Learning and Teaching, 10*(1), 80–96.

15. Orthner, D. K., Jones-Sanpei, H., Akos, P., & Rose, R. A. (2013). Improving middle school student engagement through career-relevant instruction in the core curriculum. *Journal of Educational Research, 106*(1), 27–38.

16. Williams, R. S., & Humphrey, R. (2007). Understanding and fostering interaction in threaded discussion. *Journal of Asynchronous Learning Networks, 11*(2), 129–143.

17. Alley, K. M. (2019). Fostering middle school students' autonomy to support motivation and engagement. *Middle School Journal, 50*(3), 5–14.

18. Deci, E. L., & Ryan, R. M. (2008). Facilitating optimal motivation and psychological well-being across life's domains. *Canadian Psychology, 49*(1), 14–23.

19. Steinberg, L. D., Brown, B. B., & Dornbush, S. M. (1996). *Beyond the classroom: Why school reform has failed and what parents need to do.* Simon and Schuster.

20. Deci, E. L., & Ryan, R. M. (2008). Facilitating optimal motivation and psychological well-being across life's domains. *Canadian Psychology, 49*(1), 14–23.

21. Avery, K. F. G., Huggan, C. T., & Preston, J. P. (2018). The flipped classroom: High school student engagement through 21st century learning. *In Education, 24*(1), 4–21.

22. Hellmer, S. (2012). Student autonomy and peer learning: An example. *Högre Utbildning, 2*(1), 51–54.

23. Louwrens, N., & Hartnett, M. (2015). Student and teacher perceptions of online student engagement in an online middle school. *Journal of Open, Flexible and Distance Learning, 19*(1), 27–44.

24. Cornell, D., Shukla, K., & Konold, T. R. (2016). Authoritative school climate and student academic engagement, grades, and aspirations in middle and high Schools. *AERA Open, 2*(2), 1–18.

25. Avery, K. F. G., Huggan, C. T., & Preston, J. P. (2018). The flipped classroom: High school student engagement through 21st century learning. *In Education, 24*(1), 4–21.

26. Furtak, E. M., & Kunter, M. (2012). Effects of autonomy-supportive teaching on student learning and motivation. *Journal of Experimental Education, 80*(3), 284–316.

27. Wallace, T. L., & Sung, H. C. (2017). Student perceptions of autonomy-supportive instructional interactions in the middle grades. *Journal of Experimental Education, 85*(3), 425–449.

28. Toshalis, E. (2015). *Make me! Understanding and engaging student resistance in school.* Harvard Educational Press.

29. Finn, J. D., & Rock, D. A. (1997). Academic success among students at-risk for school failure. *Journal of Applied Psychology, 82,* 221–234.

30. Furtak, E. M., & Kunter, M. (2012). Effects of autonomy-supportive teaching on student learning and motivation. *Journal of Experimental Education, 80*(3), 284–316.

31. Finn, J. D., & Rock, D. A. (1997). Academic success among students at-risk for school failure. *Journal of Applied Psychology, 82,* 221–234.

32. Blafanz, R., Fox, J., Bridgeland, J., & McNaught, M. (2009). *Grad nation: A guidebook to help communities tackle the dropout crisis.* America's Promise Alliance.

33. Perry, J. C. (2008). School engagement among urban youth of color: Criterion pattern effects of vocational exploration and racial identity. *Journal of Career Development, 34*, 397–422.

34. Alexander, K. L., Entwisle, D. R., & Horsey, C. S. (1997). From first grade forward: Early foundations of high school dropout. *Sociology of Education, 70*, 87–107.

35. Orthner, D. K., Jones-Sanpei, H., Akos, P., & Rose, R. A. (2013). Improving middle school student engagement through career-relevant instruction in the core curriculum. *Journal of Educational Research, 106*(1), 27–38.

36. Orthner, D. K., Akos, P., Rose, R., Jones-Sanpei, H., Mercado, M., & Woolley, M. (2010). CareerStart: A middle school student engagement and academic achievement program. *Children and Schools, 32*, 223–234.

37. Orthner, D. K., Cook, P., Rose, R., & Randolph, K. A. (2002). Welfare reform, poverty, and children's performance in school: Challenges for the school community. *Children and Schools, 24*, 105–121.

38. Orthner, D. K., Cook, P., Rose, R., & Randolph, K. A. (2002). Welfare reform, poverty, and children's performance in school: Challenges for the school community. *Children and Schools, 24*, 105–121.

39. Garrison, D. R., Anderson, T., & Archer, W. (2000). Critical inquiry in a text-based environment: Computer conferencing in higher education. *The Internet and Higher Education, 2*(2–3), 87–105.

Chapter 3

Transactional Distance

In the virtual environment, students rarely see their teachers in an in-person, face-to-face setting. In this setting, there is communication, mostly via live synchronous video lessons, email, text, and phone. However, teachers and students are rarely, if ever, in the same room at the same time. The distance created by the virtual environment can make teacher-student relationships much less personal than those of teachers and students in a brick-and-mortar setting. Obviously, communication is key to learning.

Although virtual teachers and students miss out on crucial opportunities for in-person interaction, most virtual schools put forth a solid effort to bridge the communication gap, utilizing live online classes, virtual meetings, online discussion boards, and video or phone conferences. Ultimately, transactional distance, as defined as the distance between two or more people as they interact, is in a virtual environment far greater than it is in a brick-and-mortar classroom.[1] It is the job of the virtual teacher to bridge that gap.

Dr. Michael G. Moore's transactional distance theory addresses the issue that I explored in this study. As virtual teachers work to create meaningful and productive relationships with their virtual students, transactional distance and its implications must be considered. In terms of this study, it was important to observe the transactional distance between students and teachers in different settings.

Application of Moore's theory happens naturally, as teachers discuss their own experiences with transactional distance and the ways it has impacted their ability to develop meaningful and productive relationships with students. Teachers in this study discussed the differences in transactional distance in each setting. They also discussed real-world methods for improving teacher-student communication in virtual settings. The concept of transactional distance is also found to be interwoven with the research on teaching presence, student engagement, students' sense of belonging, and the student's educational community. Thus, it needs to be addressed.

TREAT STUDENTS AS HUMANS

Humanization of a virtual course through deliberate acts of transactional closeness have been known to reinforce the student's acceptance in the educational community, while granting the student the confidence to become engaged in the virtual course.[2] With such a large portion of U.S. K–12 students currently attending virtual schools, it is important to think ahead to the impact transactional distance will have on these students and their future educational and professional endeavors. Attention paid to transactional distance has become crucial to all educational stakeholders; however, it is even more so in the virtual setting. At the end of the day, student success is the bottom line, and teacher-student transactional distance plays a large role in student success.

MOORE'S TRANSACTIONAL DISTANCE THEORY

To appropriately address the disparity between teacher-student relationships in brick-and-mortar settings and teacher-student relationships in virtual settings, it is imperative to discuss Moore's transactional distance theory. Moore's theory centers on the idea that the further a teacher and student are from one-another and the less communication that takes place between them, the more a student's academic achievement will suffer.[3] This theory has its roots in the ideas of Dewey and Bentley,[4] as they stressed the need for strong communication between a teacher and student. Moore first began to analyze the issue in his early work, which focused specifically on learner autonomy and independent learning and teaching.[5]

The definitive form of Moore's theory was first officially documented in 1997. This theory covered the many different forms of distance learning available at the time as part of a collection that could be similarly analyzed.[6] Moore and Bornt shared the idea that transactional distance is known to be the interactional space, either psychological or communicative, that stands between the teacher and the student.[7] Transactional distance is observable in a situation of structured or planned learning but can also apply to social or spontaneous discourse.

To understand the meaning and ultimate effectiveness of Moore's transactional distance theory in addressing the issue of distance, it is important to observe the pieces of the whole. Moore's theory was divided into three categories of observable segments in hopes of regulating the scope of transactional distance. The three clusters were identified as dialogue, structure, and learner autonomy.[8] These segments will be addressed throughout this book.

Transactional distance theory maintains that the greater the transactional distance, the less successful the virtual class.[9] Conversely, the smaller the transactional distance is found to be, the more effective the virtual class. In discussing the observed problems with distance and possible solutions to this problem, Moore stated that through the manipulation of communications media it is possible to increase dialogue between learners and their teachers and, thus, reduce the transactional distance.[10] Thus, transactional distance may be decreased through the implementation of a dedicated effort by the teacher to create more personal communication, providing students the structure and opportunity for interactions necessary to succeed.

Finally, learner autonomy is considered in Moore's theory. Learner autonomy is best revealed when the student is allowed more ownership of goals and is allowed to determine the pace and frequency of contact more so than does the teacher.[11] However, how does this work in the virtual environment? Transactional distance is also a determining factor in student autonomy.

As Garrison put it, autonomy is linked with personal responsibility, as well as with self-directedness.[12] As transactional distance increases, so do both teacher and student responsibility regarding teacher-student interactions. Ultimately, transactional distance is a measure of teacher-student communication. Thus, the virtual teacher must always consider appropriate levels of student need and autonomy when planning a lesson. Obviously, appropriate autonomy varies by student.

In discussing the importance of transactional distance, Moore shared that, especially in the virtual environment, distance between the teacher and the student often creates fissures in communication. These gaps provide a psychological space that could lead to ambiguity in teacher-student communication.[13] Thus, the teacher needs to deliberately work to decrease the transactional distance found in the virtual classroom. The closer a teacher and student are to one another in communication, the higher the rates of student success. Likewise, the greater the transactional distance, the further a teacher and student are from one another in proximity, the more limited the communication will be between them. This distance usually leads to lower academic achievement.[14]

Reduction of transactional distance in the virtual classroom must be a goal that is explicitly planned by for by the virtual teacher. Transactional distance between student and teacher is reduced when the virtual course structure encourages and requires increased dialogue and interaction. Along these lines, Garrison shared that in Moore's theory, distance creates an environment susceptible to reduced dialogue and structure.[15] Understandably then, a reduction in distance is characterized by increased dialogue and structure. This statement puts virtual school settings in the proverbial hot seat, as communication between teachers and students in a virtual environment is often much less consistent and personal than is teacher-student communication in a brick-and-mortar setting.

In a virtual classroom environment, it is rare that teachers and students communicate in person. Further, the communication that does take place in virtual settings is not typically as consistent as it is in brick-and-mortar settings. This disparity between the level of communication in the virtual classroom and that of the brick-and-mortar classroom is telling.

When teacher-student interactions are discontinuous, transactional distance increases, creating a gap in communication. This gap negatively affects student engagement and, ultimately, student academic success. There it is. Reduced transactional distance and consistent communication have been shown to improve student success, while increased transactional distance is negatively correlated with student success.

Moore's transactional distance theory is a call to action in hopes of bringing teachers and students closer together to close the transactional distance gap, thus improving student academic success. The implications of Moore's theory place virtual instruction in the spotlight, providing a path for analysis of the effectiveness of virtual education, while opening the door for exploration of the topic of teacher-student relationships.

KNOW, RESPECT, AND PLAN FOR THE GIVEN ENVIRONMENT

For a teacher to be effective in the virtual classroom, the greater transactional distance found in the virtual environment needs to be explicitly identified and taken into consideration during teacher planning.[16] It is the responsibility of the teacher to create an environment of, and opportunities for, engagement. This plan needs to be clearly communicated to the students. In fact, the idea of greater transactional distance should be openly discussed with the students in the virtual classroom. Student success also depends on the degree to which teachers involved in virtual instruction are cognizant of the ways in which students perceive their teaching presence.[17]

If a student is to be successful in a virtual environment, transactional distance between teacher and student must be reduced. The ways in which a teacher can shorten transactional distance in a virtual classroom ultimately depend on the emphasis a teacher places on presence. When a teacher plans to bridge the gap in transactional distance, and then follows through on that plan, the teacher-student relationship can flourish, allowing for greater student success. As we have seen, the transactional distance of a virtual classroom is far greater than that of a brick-and-mortar classroom. This distant dynamic, specifically known to virtual environments, also makes the formation of the teacher-student relationship more challenging than that of the in-person dynamic of a brick-and-mortar classroom.

When meaningful teacher-student interaction increases, transactional distance decreases. The onus, then, is on the teacher to facilitate student engagement that is both consequential to the student and academically effective. Much of the existing research regarding online student engagement has focused primarily on behavioral engagement.[18] The existing research shows that student engagement that is virtual and both social and academic has seldom been the focus of study. One hope of this book is to bridge that gap.

UNWRITTEN RULES

When observed side by side, the unwritten rules of teacher-student interaction differ between those of a brick-and-mortar classroom and those of a virtual environment. In looking at the two primary classroom settings, a critical factor of effective teaching in any model has been found to be student engagement. However, in dissecting the two models, research has found the virtual environment to be organized by a different protocol of rules than is typically observed in the brick-and-mortar model.[19] Although student engagement may be nurtured through questioning, virtual students may find ways to avoid answering questions.

Based on my experience, the idea of some students avoiding engagement by "hiding" during a virtual class is an absolute reality. In a virtual setting, questions are more easily ignored online than in a brick-and mortar setting. Ultimately, the increased transactional distance of the virtual setting makes it easier for a student to avoid answering the teacher. When confronted with this situation, it is incumbent on the teacher to change methods of communication and interaction to better accommodate communication.

I have also found that phone calls and parent-teacher conferences help to reinvigorate student attendance and participation. This is especially helpful when a student is unresponsive due to playing video games instead of paying attention to class. Although it has been accurately observed that teacher presence is instrumental to student learning, it has been conversely discovered that student engagement has the ability to impact teacher presence either positively or negatively.[20] This shows the symbiotic reality of the teacher-student relationship, as student engagement is a driving factor in teacher engagement. Indeed, a great deal of teacher presence comes down to "reading the room" and making adjustments as needed. The participants in this study concurred with this assessment.

The challenge of transactional distance needs to be explicitly identified and taken into consideration during teacher planning. Regardless of setting, but especially in the virtual classroom, it is the responsibility of the teacher to create an environment of, and opportunities for, engagement. This plan needs to be clearly communicated to the students. When the transactional distance gap is bridged in planning, students are better able to thrive.

TEACHERS ADDRESS TRANSACTIONAL DISTANCE

In discussing the challenges associated with reducing the transactional distance between teacher and student in the virtual classroom, the participants in this study shared stories, methods, theories, and classroom activities aimed at bridging the transactional distance gap known specifically to virtual education.

TRANSACTIONAL DISTANCE IN VIRTUAL ENVIRONMENTS AS OPPOSED TO BRICK-AND-MORTAR SETTINGS

The virtual classroom produces a greater transactional distance than does the brick-and-mortar classroom. The participants in this study discussed the challenges presented by an environment in which in-person communication rarely, if ever, takes place. On this topic, Jill discussed the differences between the virtual and brick-and-mortar environments when she shared:

> So, in a brick-and-mortar, there's two different things that I think happens. Number one, there's a captive audience, right? Here, teachers have domain over them. I'll use seventh grade as an example of seventh grade teachers. When they're with you those forty-five minutes, you can ensure because you can physically see them that they don't have phones out. They don't have their friend's notes out. So cheating is much more limited. What gets blocked [in the virtual environment] is the classroom management piece, right? You can do a lot of things to encourage, but they're smart. And they know how to slow down the pace of the schedule.

In discussing her greatest transactional distance challenge, Jill stated:

> My biggest struggle is them being allowed to just shut me off, for lack of better words, right? . . . they're shutting off learning, right? That's not okay. We should never allow students in any way, shape or form to shut off learning, period. . . . if they were in a brick-and-mortar, those not engaging or absences, they would've been in truancy right away, right?

To Jill, many students need the brick-and mortar experience, as they are not self-disciplined enough to effectively utilize the autonomy that is a real part of the virtual classroom. Similarly, Joy stated:

> There has to be this consistent flow of communication, and any time you start to see like I don't remember seeing that kid for a couple days, or I don't remember hearing from that learning coach after that last email, then you've got to start doing extra work.

Joy's discussion on her experience with transactional distance in both the brick-and-mortar and the virtual environment brought her to the point of discussing situations in which the virtual environment might not be the best setting for a given student. On this issue, Joy stated:

> I don't think we need to make this school work for every single student. So, if they're here, then they have made an agreement and their parents have made an agreement for them, but they are in a situation where they need to pull their weight. . . . and if these parameters don't work for you, this might not be the best environment.

Joy discussed working in the now defunct VIVA program, Community Day. Community Day was a program in which students would attend a live class in a brick-and-mortar setting for half a school day, once a week, and then attend virtual school the rest of the week. Here, teachers and students could see each other in-person and could really get to know one another.

I taught Community Day for several years and can testify to its effectiveness. The teachers, parents, and students really enjoyed the program. Joy found this program to bring a nice balance to the program, as it supplemented the virtual classroom with an in-person component. While lamenting the ending of the program, Joy reminisced regarding the advantages of the reduction of transactional distance Community Day provided.

> I miss Community Day so much, because Community Day was like this beautiful blend of independence with these islands in the middle of the week where you could talk to parents and you could see the kids and you could read their body language and you could look at physical work and get that immediate feedback. . . . My favorite thing about Community Day was that I could walk around a classroom and connect with each student, even if it was just sharing a look for a moment, looking down at their paper, putting my hand on their shoulder if they were doing something different or tapping their desk just to remind them this is what we're doing right now. I miss that piece, that physical proximity piece.

Ultimately, Community Day acted as a once per week check-in. It provided a beneficial bridge in transactional distance.

Similar to Joy, Karen longed for the personal connection of the brick-and-mortar setting. Karen discussed the intangibles that are more difficult to ascertain in a virtual classroom than in a brick-and-mortar setting. Those intangibles to Karen really helped to inform communication, thus lessening teacher-student transactional distance. Karen shared:

> Whereas in a brick and mortar, there's all that extra information that you can get kind of by looking at what the student looks like, what they're wearing every day, the things that they bring to school with them, what they eat, all that other information that helps you figure out what kind of person or what the kids are into.

What Karen brings to the discussion here is an explanation of those little personal attributes of a student that are more difficult to observe in a virtual environment than in a brick-and-mortar setting. Observations made in person definitely aid in the formation of meaningful and productive teacher-student relationships, again, underscoring the challenges presented on this front in terms of building personal relationships in the virtual setting.

Bobbi's take on transactional distance in a virtual environment was strikingly similar to that of Karen. Bobbi shared:

> This is one of the hard things about online learning, right? When I was in a classroom, even just as a student teacher, you could see what work the student was doing, which you can see partially at VIVA, too. You could see which student walked in and was just a mess from the get-go. They'd walk in and by 8:15, they're already crying over something that probably didn't happen at school. And you're right there to be the mediator and the problem solver, and whatever you need to be, and I feel like that distance is obviously a little bigger at VIVA.
>
> So, our job has to be to shorten it a little bit, or make it a little bit less distant, which I think is a bigger feat and I think the whole world figured that out during COVID. It's a bigger feat at an online school than it would be a brick-and-mortar school.

Through recollections of her experience, Bobbi identified the need to shorten the transactional distance in the virtual environment. Here again, the virtual teacher longs for the experience of actually seeing the students, getting a read on body language, and using the brick-and-mortar classroom setting as a place to assist the students with any perceived issues that might affect the student emotionally or academically.

Daisy also talked about the challenges of transactional distance, specifically that found in the virtual environment, as compared to that of a brick-and-mortar classroom. Communication was discussed as the definitive solution to student disengagement. She also talked in detail regarding issues she has faced with students disconnecting in the virtual setting. Daisy shared:

> Well, brick and mortar, you're there with them. You're in close proximity. You're not just behind a computer screen and you're there with them more than three hours a day. So, I mean, we get the feel as virtual teachers what their challenges are and what their strengths are, but being in a closer proximity, obviously, you know firsthand that they are either focused or not focused and you know if they are getting it or not getting it because with the virtual environment, some of the kids actually are getting it, but you might think aren't, but they're just quiet. They're not as interactive. . . . When you're in close proximity in the brick and mortar, you see those people. There's kids [in the virtual environment] I haven't even seen, there's parents I haven't even seen, but you just have to communicate. That's why it's so important to reach out to these families constantly that we don't really have time to do and just bridge that gap that way. I mean, that's all we can really do.

Daisy's frustration with the inability to personally monitor the students is clear. However, she continues to implement strategies to reduce transactional distance in the virtual classroom.

Like Daisy, Michelle identified the differences in transactional distance between the brick-and-mortar setting and the virtual setting, sharing that the virtual environment requires more teacher effort to reduce the transactional distance between the teacher and the student. Michelle stated:

> With virtual, it requires more work. With brick and mortar, the kids are right there. You can build that relationship and that transaction between teacher and student to be kind of immediate, whereas virtual they're not right there. You can't physically see them unless their cameras are on, they're in Zoom or whatever. But you have to be intentional about sending those emails and calling and sending in those chats and whatever. At least for a virtual setting it's me. For me at least, it requires a little more work to build that transaction, to build that relationship in a virtual setting than it would, probably, brick and mortar.

Continuing, Michelle shared the idea that virtual setting offers students a much easier path to disengage than does the brick-and-mortar setting. She stated:

> Brick and mortar, they have to be in the class, and they have to be there whether they're going to check in or engage or not. That's one thing. But with the virtual, if they don't feel like welcomed or they don't feel like the teacher cares, they could easily just not click into Blackboard. Especially in a virtual environment.

Mike talked about the importance of seeing students in person, though he shared the idea that it is indeed possible to build that relationship without seeing them regularly. Mike stated:

> I think just the simple fact that the student can see the teacher and the teacher can see the student has made a difference, even if it's just one time. Doesn't necessarily mean that it has to be all the time. . . . But the fact that I can see my students [on camera], especially the ones that do engage readily, and I think that's made a difference.

Continuing, Mike shared his ideas on reasons students disengage, citing previous school settings as a possible cause. He shared:

> Even students who didn't necessarily have a good experience in brick and mortar, we tend to get them, and a lot of times you're trying to undo whatever experience that they had before. That takes a while as well.

Each of the participants in this study identified transactional distance in the virtual environment as a challenge. As a follow-up to the definition of the problem, the participants discussed ways in which the transactional distance may be shortened in the virtual school setting.

HOW DO YOU REDUCE TRANSACTIONAL DISTANCE?

Reduction of teacher-student transactional distance in the virtual school setting was identified by each participant as a considerable challenge in the ongoing struggle to build meaningful and productive teacher-student relationships. In discussing the techniques she regularly utilizes to reduce transactional distance, Jill talked about virtual whiteboards that students may use to complete written work, while the teacher supervises in real time.

> One of the ones [virtual whiteboards] that's come out in PLC is called Whiteboard.Fi, and I love using that because I can see what they're writing on the whiteboard at the same time, and nobody else can see it except for me. But it gives me that feeling like in the classroom when I say: "Okay, write this stuff down on your whiteboard and show it to me." That's the piece that's missing for me in virtual education is that one-on-one connection. Even in a roomful of kids, you feel like you're getting that one-on-one transaction. And it's missing in virtual education to be sure.

As someone who has utilized Whiteboard.fi, I agree with Jill and can testify to its intuitiveness. I would, however, recommend that teachers insist that students use their own names in whiteboard, as the names can get silly and distracting. Plus, it's good to know who is working with each whiteboard.

Karen's techniques for connecting with students included seeing them in person (before COVID) and utilizing web cameras with students and parents.

> So, I mean, one of the things I really liked to do before the pandemic was to actually set up times where I could see students in person. I feel like even if you see somebody in person for just a small amount of time, that can help reduce the transactional distance. And I think we very much used to not have cameras on during classes. So, I'd say the two things that I think can reduce transactional distance in teacher-student relationships is just kind of physically seeing what each other looks like.
>
> So, when we have those conferences or we have opportunities to use cameras in classes, that's helpful. . . .

Short of being able to connect either in person or through a web camera, Karen shared other manners of communication that she has found to be successful in bridging the transactional distance gap. Karen stated:

> So, if I don't hear or I'm not able to build that relationship with a student during class, I try to change it up by sending them an email instead, sending them a text or a phone call because some students just really don't do well with the online tools that we have. But they might be better at texting or phone calls or emails, for whatever reason. . . . There's a lot more resistance I think for that kind of chatting with the teacher . . . there's more resistance online than there is in a brick-and-mortar setting.

Mike shared similar views with Karen to seeing families in person as a remedy for the transactional distance that challenges virtual teachers. Again, he did not feel that teachers and students needed to necessarily see one another in person regularly. Mike shared:

> In years prior, I had a few students that would attend every outing. You build that relationship and then you take it to your virtual environment, and it tends to carry over.

Bobbi discussed techniques for getting through to students who might not willingly share their needs, concerns, or shortcomings, especially in a virtual setting. Bobbi stated:

> I think just encouraging that [discussion] more than in a brick-and-mortar is super important because you can't necessarily see, especially when we're not on video, who's having a bad day. I have no idea if they're just sitting there with their name on the screen. Yeah, maybe you call on them and they don't answer

and that's weird, but you don't know what's going on unless they tell you, so you have to make them want to tell you.

Finally, Daisy stated that she despises being on camera but finds it be a necessary evil in reaching the students on a personal level.

> One thing that I'm terrible about, as you know, is being on camera. I don't like it. I can't stand it, but that's one way.

Each teacher recognized the challenges in bridging the transactional distance gap in the virtual classroom. The data from this study found that it is easier for students to disengage in the virtual setting, than in a brick-and-mortar setting. In the brick-and-mortar setting, the teacher actually sees the students in person, whereas in the virtual setting, if they wish, students are able to turn off microphones and cameras.

Although teachers in the virtual environment know these matters all too well, each teacher offered suggestions for reducing the transactional distance gap and for building meaningful and productive teacher-student relationships in the virtual school environment.

This distance in interaction between students and teachers is known as transactional distance. The goal of the teachers in this study was repeatedly stated as being the reduction of transactional distance, thus bridging the gap that exists in teacher-student interactions in the virtual setting.

A RECOGNITION OF THE REALITY OF THE SIGNIFICANT TRANSACTIONAL DISTANCE FOUND IN THE VIRTUAL ENVIRONMENT

Transactional distance is defined as the distance between two or more people as they interact. This distance is reduced the closer the people are to one another as they interact and is widened the farther they are apart. Given the nature of both the brick-and-mortar and the virtual setting, it is clear that a greater transactional distance is found in the virtual setting. Both the literature and the stories of the participants supported this notion.

The participants supported the idea that the brick-and-mortar environment allows for a captive audience of students in which a teacher can watch, in person, students as they work and interact with others, as opposed to the virtual environment in which there is little to no in-person interaction and in which the interactions that do occur are limited to what is observable within the range of the camera lens.

Participants in this study shared that the transactional distance in the virtual environment at VIVA is greater than it would be in a brick-and-mortar setting. Some of the participants, such as Bobbi, shared that one of the main jobs of the virtual teacher must be to shorten the transactional distance, while recognizing that a reduction in transactional distance is indeed a bigger feat at a virtual school than it would be in a brick-and-mortar school. Jill stated that the virtual environment demands a: "consistent flow of communication," necessary to keep ahead of and reduce the widened transactional distance found in the virtual environment.

Similarly, Karen discussed the extra information that can be attained through in-person observation, such as: "what the student looks like, what they're wearing every day, the things that they bring to school with them, what they eat, all that other information that helps you figure out what kind of person or what the kids are into." In addressing the disparity in transactional distance between the virtual classroom and the brick-and-mortar classroom, Daisy discussed proximity, stating:

> Well, brick and mortar, you're there with them. You're in close proximity. You're not just behind a computer screen and you're there with them more than three hours a day. So, I mean, we get the feel as virtual teachers what their challenges are and what their strengths are, but being in a closer proximity, obviously, you know firsthand that they are either focused or not focused and you know if they are getting it or not getting it.

The teachers in this study understood and recognized the difference in transactional distance in the virtual environment as opposed to that of the brick-and-mortar setting. Not seeing students in person each day was identified as the key reason for the widened transactional distance of the virtual classroom environment. The literature on transactional distance in virtual settings supports the findings of the participants in this study.

The literature on transactional distance confirmed the findings of the participants, offering that transactional distance in the virtual environment is far greater than that of a brick-and-mortar classroom, as virtual teachers and students rarely or never see one another in person.

Research has displayed the importance of reducing the transactional distance, as the success of a virtual class relies on a lessening of transactional distance in teacher-student interactions. In discussing problems with the widened transactional distance of virtual environments, researchers have discovered that gaps in transactional distance sometimes provide an emotional gap that leaves the student susceptible to ambiguity in teacher-student communication, as the virtual environment inherently invites ambiguity in communication more so than does the brick-and-mortar setting. This gap negatively affects student engagement and, ultimately, student academic success.

The literature supports the data created through the storytelling of the teachers. The transactional distance of the virtual environment is greater than that of a brick-and-mortar environment. Because of this reality, teachers in the virtual environment must place more focus and energy on reducing this distance than do their brick-and-mortar counterparts. A reduction in transactional distance is necessary for student academic success, as well as in keeping the student from drifting emotionally, as the virtual environment is often a lonely and isolating place. Both the literature and the narratives of the participants reinforce this point. Ultimately, if a student is to succeed academically, the teacher-student connection must be established early and reinforced regularly, especially in a virtual school setting.

NARROWING THE SIGNIFICANT TRANSACTIONAL DISTANCE FOUND IN THE VIRTUAL ENVIRONMENT

The significant and clearly observed gaps in the transactional distance of the virtual middle school classroom environment were found in both the literature and by the participants in this study to be one of the main challenges in the building of meaningful and productive teacher-student relationships in the virtual middle school environment. It is through the planning for presence and the facilitation of opportunities for teacher-student and student-student connections that the transactional distance of the virtual environment can begin to be reduced.

The reduction of transactional distance has been found to be key to the building of teacher-student relationships, as well as being vital to student academic success. To take on the challenges brought forth by the virtual classroom model, teachers need to be aware of the realities of the widened transactional distance inherent in virtual environments, as this gap has been found to negatively affect student engagement and, ultimately, student academic success. In closing, or decreasing, this gap, virtual middle school teachers may facilitate learning in a more productive manner. Although the in-person transactional distance of the brick-and-mortar classroom will always be smaller than that of the virtual environment, it is possible, through planning for social presence and the creation of opportunities for connection, to narrow that gap. Transactional distance should be considered in the virtual teacher's planning. Activities geared toward reducing this gap should be utilized if a teacher is to build meaningful and productive teacher-student relationships and facilitate student academic success in the virtual middle school environment.

FROM THE PD!

How Do You Bridge the Transactional Distance Gap in the Virtual Environment?

Encourage participation, polls
Show up to class using a funny image on Snap Cam
Meet with students in small groups and speak individually with them . . . lots of questioning!
introducing siblings and pets
We welcome and say hello to all on camera
Lots of time to share and interact in smaller groups
I have my own kids share their thoughts with the students
Notes to the camera. dog/cats to camera. Ceiling cam.
Work on students interacting with each other with mics/cameras.
I follow up weekly with students in individual breakout rooms on their hobbies or events that they shared out previously in the year.
I normalize not having it all together.
Cameras, reach out to students who say they aren't having a good day, make phone calls

How Do You Allow Students to Get to Know You?

HUMAN Aspect
Yes, share your regular home life in class. It helps them see that you are a real person.
I share my cringe school day stories, so they know we all go through it :)
When you have actual conversations like that they see you as a person like them and they will share too.
I play a music video
We have been at the fall coffee shop
I do music too. I like it
Love word find!
Lots of pet parades too
I am passionate about history, so I do "today in history" and we talk about it.
rule is pets MUST be shown!
I have a student lead homeroom
I share anecdotes about my boys, so they know I am human too and that I can relate to them because I go through it all with my kids.
We just had a student's dog have puppies—she has been sharing one in class every day—we are loving it

They worked on their research reports together in class yesterday and just listened to jazz. It was awesome!

Fridays we do "show me something" like pets, siblings, something cool near you, etc.

Kids need to feel safe

I play impromptu games of camera on camera off if I see a lot of cameras off. That way some of them leave them on after.

I do team drawing

They look forward to Chit Chat Friday in my Homeroom.

We have been doing the Wayside School stories and have a raffle on Fridays

I do hallway hangouts in homeroom a lot, they love it, and I change up what they do. I do topic chat, mini mysteries, and QOTD

These are the tips and tricks shared by our teachers. I hope you find some of the ideas presented here useful and helpful. I will include discussions such as these in each segment of this book. Next, we will examine teacher presence.

NOTES

1. Moore, M. (1993). Theory of transactional distance. In D. Keegan, ed., *Theoretical Principles of Distance Education* (1st ed., pp. 22–38). Routledge.

2. Collins, K., Grroff, S., Mathena, C., & Kupczynski, L. (2019). Asynchronous video and the development of instructor social presence and student engagement. *Turkish Online Journal of Distance Education, 20*(1), 53–70.

3. Moore, M. (1993). Theory of transactional distance. In D. Keegan, ed., *Theoretical Principles of Distance Education* (1st ed., pp. 22–38). Routledge.

4. Dewey, J., & Bentley, A. (1949). *Knowing and the known.* Beacon Press.

5. Moore, M. G. (1972). Learner autonomy: The second dimension of independent learning. *Convergence, 5*(2), 76–88.

6. Bornt, D. (2011). *Moore's theory of transactional distance: Instructional design models, theories & methodology.* www.k3hamilton.com/LTech/transactional.html

7. Bornt, D. (2011). *Moore's theory of transactional distance: Instructional design models, theories & methodology.* www.k3hamilton.com/LTech/transactional.html

8. Bornt, D. (2011). *Moore's theory of transactional distance: Instructional design models, theories & methodology.* www.k3hamilton.com/LTech/transactional.html

9. Forte, G., Schwandt, D., Swayze, S., Butler, J., & Ashcraft, M. (2016). Distance education in the U.S.: A paradox. *Turkish Online Journal of Distance Education, 17*(3). http://doi.org/10.17718/tojde.95102

10. Moore, M. (1997). Theory of transactional distance. In D. Keegan, ed., *Theoretical Principles of Distance Education* (2nd ed., pp. 22–38). Routledge.

11. Moore, M. (1997). Theory of transactional distance. In D. Keegan, ed., *Theoretical Principles of Distance Education* (2nd ed., pp. 22–38). Routledge.

12. Garrison, D. R. (2000). Theoretical challenges for distance education in the 21st century: A shift from structural to transactional issues. *The International Review of Research in Open and Distributed Learning, 1*(1). https://doi.org/10.19173/irrodl.v1i1.2

13. Moore, M., & Kearsley, G. (1996). *Distance education: A systems review.* Wadsworth Publishing Company.

14. Kucuk, S., & Richardson, J. C. (2019). A structural equation model of predictors of online learners' engagement and satisfaction. *Online Learning, 23*(2), 196–216.

15. Garrison, D. R. (2000). Theoretical challenges for distance education in the 21st century: A shift from structural to transactional issues. *The International Review of Research in Open and Distributed Learning, 1*(1). https://doi.org/10.19173/irrodl.v1i1.2

16. Marks, R. B., Sibley, S. D., & Arbaugh, J. B. (2005). A structural equation model of predictors for effective online learning. *Journal of Management Education, 29*(10) 531–563.

17. Ekmekci, O. (2013). Being there: Establishing presence in an online learning environment. *Higher Education Studies, 3*(1), 29–38. https://doi.org/10.5539/hes.v3n1p29

18. Louwrens, N., & Hartnett, M. (2015). Student and teacher perceptions of online student engagement in an online middle school. *Journal of Open, Flexible and Distance Learning, 19*(1), 27–44.

19. Lapadat, J. C. (2007). Discourse devices used to establish community, increase coherence, and negotiate agreement in an online university course. *The Journal of Distance Education, 21*(3), 59–92.

20. Gray, J. A., & DiLoreto, M. (2016). The effects of student engagement, student satisfaction, and perceived learning in online learning environments. *International Journal of Educational Leadership Preparation, 11*(1), n1.

Chapter 4

Teacher Presence

Middle school teachers who work in a virtual setting have more difficulty in building relationships with students than do teachers in a brick-and-mortar setting. This is a seemingly obvious observation that is backed by my experience teaching in the virtual middle school setting. When a teacher and student do not see one another in person, it certainly is more difficult to build relationships than it is in a brick-and-mortar setting.

The building of teacher-student relationships depends on teacher presence, both social and academic, with a healthy push needed in the direction of teacher social presence. The construction of these social relationships is crucial, as teacher presence is known to be a factor in the academic success of students. Teachers who see their students in person each day are better able to interact, understand, and relate to students than are virtual teachers who interact primarily online.[1] Although many virtual schools utilize camera-based programs in which the students and teacher interact, the in-person component is missing from the virtual classroom.

A virtual setting does not allow for the same kinds of interactions as does a brick-and-mortar setting. Simply seeing a student each day and observing the student's body language, how that student walks into a room, interacts with other students, and with the teacher, socially, how the student is dressed, and so on are all pieces of the puzzle that are difficult to attain virtually. An obstacle in virtual education is the embedded absence of in-person teacher-student communication.[2]

Teacher presence has shown itself to be a critical component of student success. The process of piquing student interest and stimulating intellectual curiosity encompasses all teacher-student interactions, including social exchanges and lesson follow-ups outside of class.[3] Similarly, every teacher-student interaction contributes to overall teaching presence.[4] Further, the real efforts made in developing virtual teacher-student relationships positively impact student engagement, bringing the teacher and student closer together, as well as bringing the student closer to the curriculum, ultimately fostering student success. Although student interactions with content and peers are crucial in nurturing the student's overall success, the construction of the meaningful and productive teacher-student relationship is vital to the establishment of the positive learning environment.[5]

While brick-and-mortar classrooms offer many teacher opportunities for student engagement, such as in-person collaborations and working closely in person with students to stimulate intellectual curiosity, providing for similar opportunities in the virtual environment can be challenging. Success is partially contingent on the development of student sense of belonging, which must be fostered by the teacher.[6] Even small changes in the ways the teacher interacts as a human and not as an authority figure, with shows of respect given to the student, and the student's input, truly do matter to the student, as those changes encourage increased positive participation and students' sense of belonging. Given the correlation found between teacher presence and student satisfaction and success, it is reasonable to state that teacher presence wields a heavy hand in influencing learning.[7]

Positive academic outcomes tend to hinge on teacher presence.[8] Students who enjoy a strong and consistent teaching presence in the virtual environment are more likely to be satisfied with courses than those students who do not.[9] Along these lines, students learning in a virtual environment have stated that live classes, including direct instruction from a teacher, were more meaningful and productive than classes that are designed for students to be simply left alone to complete assignments.[10] The idea of teacher presence as a driving force for student academic achievement and satisfaction was a key topic of study in my research.

As it has become apparent that two determining factors of student success have been found to be teacher presence and student engagement, the significance of the link between student success and teacher-student relationships has become clearer. When looking at the issue through the lens of virtual education and K–12 virtual academies, new questions arise regarding the challenges surrounding teacher presence and student engagement in a virtual classroom environment. The literature here describes teacher-student relationships as being crucial to student engagement and learning.

In looking at the relationship between teacher presence and student engagement, it is necessary for a teacher in a virtual setting to come to an understanding regarding the differences in the realities of virtual learning versus brick-and-mortar learning, as well as recognizing productive procedures that tend to foster increased student engagement in the virtual classroom. Productive teacher-student relationships promoted engagement among the learners. When students are engaged, teacher-student relationships may be built on a solid foundation. Likewise, when teachers facilitate opportunities for meaningful and productive teacher-student relationships, student engagement usually increases.

Teaching presence is both a key factor in the construction of teacher-student relationships and in the facilitation of student academic success, yet when discussed in the context of the virtual classroom, the classic idea of teaching presence changes dramatically, as presence takes on a new, and less literal, meaning. Before the advent of virtual classrooms, teaching presence was defined as the design, facilitation, and direction of cognitive and social processes for realizing personally meaningful and educationally worthwhile learning outcomes.[11] Although some tenets of the previous understanding of teacher presence remain untouched, others have shifted to meet the ever-changing models of modern education. Teaching presence has been described as the force that establishes and fosters a critical community of inquiry, as it has been discovered that the formation of student cognitive presence and social presence depend largely on the presence of a teacher.[12] The teacher, then, is acting as facilitator, bringing together academic and social presence through the act of deliberately establishing teacher presence in all aspects of teaching, from planning to teaching to following up with students after a given lesson.

When discussing the effects of teacher presence on student academic success, we have learned that teaching presence has predicted student academic achievement and student course satisfaction.[13] Similarly, it has been discovered that teaching presence is vital in the cultivation of student satisfaction and success. Deliberate teacher presence, when planned for and utilized by the teacher, is known to be a determining factor in student achievement.

Although the connection between teacher presence and student success might seem evident, virtual classrooms know a much less personal, less hands-on, and more distant dynamic than that of in-person teacher presence in a brick-and-mortar setting. Teaching presence is most effective when it includes close observation and the facilitation of purposeful collaborations and reflections.[14] The lack of in-person teaching presence, indicative of virtual environments, and increased transactional distance found in virtual schools places this model at a distinct disadvantage, as virtual schools are unable to provide the same kind of direct feedback and immediate student support found in brick-and-mortar school settings. Virtual teachers must then be deliberate in their plans for and execution of teacher presence.

In discussing teacher presence, it is important to consider the notion that the concept of teacher presence is as old as the idea of teachers teaching students. In looking at the historic considerations of such ideas, I must discuss John Dewey. Dewey[15] defined presence as the act of teachers being fully attentive to students' cognitive reactions. Whether viewed through the lens of a brick-and-mortar classroom or a virtual classroom, Dewey's basic idea of teacher-presence, and its evident implications on teacher-student relationships, remains relevant today. Ultimately, some teaching presence is automatic, some is planned, some is spontaneous, and some is social, but each piece of teacher presence plays into the bigger idea of the formation of effective, enduring teacher-student relationships.

TEACHING PRESENCE AS A DELIBERATE ACT

Teacher-student interaction is vital to student success in any setting, but if a teacher is to bridge the transactional distance gap that exists in the virtual setting, the teacher in a virtual setting must place extra emphasis on presence. Teacher presence is most useful when utilized as an explicit piece of a virtual lesson plan, as presence is paramount to the overall lesson. A teacher's online presence is most productive when it creates an opportunity for student engagement.[16] This is a task that falls squarely at the feet of the teacher in a virtual setting. How does a teacher's planning, both academic and social, nurture the opportunity for engagement? Every person teaching in a virtual setting should address this question.

Not unlike lesson planning in brick-and-mortar settings, teaching presence is most meaningful when it ensures that intended learning outcomes are reached. Here, teacher presence is being used as a teaching tool. Along these lines, it has been regularly noted that attention to teacher social and academic presence relates directly to matters regarding class management, teacher-student, small group and whole class discussions, and instruction.[17] In the context of the virtual classroom, teacher presence is multidimensional, as teachers must create and implement a plan that fosters the creation of and continued bolstering of teacher-student communication. Planned meaningful and productive teacher-student interaction allows the student to feel connected to the teacher, thus aiding in student sense of belonging and, ultimately, in positive student academic success. This connection is not simple, as its complex makeup reaches beyond the act of simply being physically present. Thus, it is up to the teacher to create an environment of, and opportunities for, engagement.

Given the challenges of teaching in a virtual environment, the role of the instructor in enabling online learners' success has been deemed critical.[18] Overall, a great deal of virtual teacher presence is most effective when it is a deliberately arranged piece of a teacher's lesson plans. Thus, the acts of planning and the setting of high expectations, in terms of both academics and interactions, are crucial components to the virtual learning experience.

Even with careful planning, it can be difficult to fully gauge whether a student is being impacted by a teacher in a virtual environment. Teachers in virtual settings should be cognizant of the ways in which their teaching presence is realized and appreciated by students, as the learning experience of the student is largely dependent on meaningful teacher, social, and academic presence.[19] Thus, teacher presence should be deliberately analyzed through critical reflection. To diminish the cruciality of teacher presence is to overlook the significance of the critical binding of social activities with those activities that are academic in nature. The most effective tools for real teacher-student communication are often found in the planning itself.

SEGMENTS OF TEACHING PRESENCE

The concept of teaching presence is not linear, and it is not limited to a perfect answer or possibility. In fact, teaching presence may be divided into several observable pieces. In considering the range of the segments of teaching presence, research has shown that the main segments of teaching presence include design and organization, facilitation of discussion, and direct instruction.[20] When teaching presence is deconstructed further and utilized with the different segments of presence, it becomes clear that when at one with social presence and academic presence, teaching presence creates and contributes to a collaborative community of inquiry and effective learning.[21]

SOCIAL PRESENCE

Although it can be a difficult undertaking, meaningful and productive teacher-student relationships may be formed in virtual environments if a teacher is effective in planning for such. A major piece of that planning is the incorporation of social presence. Teaching presence includes the teacher's social actions within the virtual environment in a manner that provides consequential and educationally useful learning experiences and results for the students.

In general, teaching practices that are recommended for excellent educational experiences must include dedicated connections with students, planning for and encouraging opportunities for peer collaboration, the promotion of active learning, the offering of timely and supportive feedback, communication, and follow-through of high expectations, and the fashioning of individualized educational paths with special attention paid to each student's work and life experiences.[22] The focus on great expectations is crucial to student success, as it is through the communication of shared goals, teacher and student accountability, and elevated expectations that the teacher is able to facilitate an unrestricted conversation while inspiring teacher-student and student-student teamwork.[23]

Social presence is a new piece of the overall breakdown of teacher presence.[24] Often, social presence is discussed along with teaching presence, as it is the visibility and actions of an involved and effectual virtual teacher that often encourages student engagement. Thus, teacher presence extends to the teacher's social actions, as well as the teacher's virtual reach in assessing student work and giving feedback. Student social engagement often nurtures student academic engagement. This is true of both brick-and-mortar and virtual classroom environments but is especially crucial to the success of virtual students.[25]

Along these lines, research has uncovered that a focus on deliberate teacher-planned opportunities to participate in online interactions has been connected to improved social presence.[26] Teacher expectations need to be clear and consistent. Teacher academic and social support have each become connected to student engagement, as well as whole child development.[27] Although teacher presence is one of several pieces of the construction of the teacher-student relationship, it is the many subdivisions of presence that make it whole.

The personal and professional strands of teacher presence in terms of social presence are best understood when first acknowledged and then deconstructed. In terms of the importance of teacher social presence, Dewey[28] shared the idea that education is a social process that requires members of a learning community to cooperate as they problem solve together. To address the divisions that make social presence whole, Whiteside unveiled the social presence model.[29]

THE SOCIAL PRESENCE MODEL

The social presence model is a living construct that suggests social presence consists of the following five integrated elements: affective association, community cohesion, instructor involvement, interaction intensity, and knowledge and experience.[30] This is a thorough consideration of teacher-student social interaction. In utilizing this model, researchers have discovered that whether or not teachers know about the social presence model, they largely value its segments and view it as an essential new experiential measure for the facilitation of improved student academic success.[31] Teaching presence with a focus on social presence in a blended, partially virtual approach is helpful to students in terms of self-directed and cooperative critical thinking and problem solving.[32]

Transcending its identity as one of many tools, the social presence model has been characterized as a new literacy that is critical to the attainment of a successful virtual learning environment.[33] Ultimately, when visibility and activity come in the form of a virtual classroom, a teacher must be proactive in communicating expectations, as well as feedback, with the student.

TEACHER ENCOURAGEMENT OF STUDENTS

I am going to, once again, bring up the quote (Was it Maxwell? Was it Theodore Roosevelt? Was it etc . . . ?) I used previously in the book. I will do this again later, as it so well encapsulates the big idea. That saying is as follows: *Students don't care what you know, until they know you care.* When it comes to teacher-student relationship building, positive human connections are crucial to productive outcomes. Inasmuch as deliberate teacher planning is immensely important, it has been my experience that for teaching virtually to be effective, teaching presence observed by the student should be optimistic, pleasant, competent, thoughtful, and steady.

If the student feels that the teacher cares about their success, that student will tend to perform better academically. Ultimately, mutual respect between the teacher and student is a fundamental factor in the building of meaningful and productive teacher-student relationships. When the input of students is encouraged, appreciated, and identified as valuable, students are more likely to be inspired to proactively complete coursework. Presence, accessibility, and the reassuring nature of a teacher each significantly influence the student engagement and sense of belonging, while helping to shape a meaningful virtual school experience.[34] Acting as and being perceived as a decent human being is key to the building of teacher-student relationships.

A teacher working to maximize social presence in a virtual setting can promote a meaningful and productive virtual classroom environment. Thus, teachers need to be engaged with, caring for, and visible to their students from start to finish. Related to this idea, the results of a study conducted by Jackson, Jones, and Rodriguez[35] found that students tend to be satisfied with virtual courses when teachers work to create a meaningful teacher-student relationship and a productive classroom environment. Student expectations of teacher presence confirm findings that point to teacher performance as a key element in teaching presence.[36] The utilization of teacher social presence is important in getting through to students in a way that may result in student success. It is important for a student to feel that a teacher cares and is actively involved in the learning process, because this could ultimately be the difference between a successful student and a failing student.

SPECIFIC TEACHER LANGUAGE

Words matter. Teacher social presence may enhance a student's learning experience in a virtual setting through the utilization of specific language. The cultivation of social presence and the act of unambiguously showing respect to students hinges on proper word usage. Further, using phrases such as: *I need you to . . . , you will want to . . . , and to have the opportunity to be successful you must . . .* help to facilitate unguarded interaction.[37] Further, using I-messages and other pronouns coupled with an informal quality while speaking with encouragement often cultivates a supportive classroom environment.[38] Students listen to the exact words of teachers. It is crucial that teachers choose their words and phrases carefully. When teachers task students to choose words wisely, it is incumbent on the teacher to do the same.

Teacher presence is a key concept in the creation of and stability of teacher-student relationships and in the nurturing of student academic success. Exactly how teacher presence is approached in a virtual environment differs greatly from that of a brick-and-mortar classroom and must be planned for accordingly.

Social presence is a key component of teacher presence because the visibility and actions of an involved and teacher who teaches virtually have been found to lead to greater student academic achievement. In 1938, Dewey shared the idea that education is social, as it requires interaction allowing for collaboration between students and teachers.[39] Teaching practices that are highlighted by strong connections with students, planning for and facilitating the opportunities for peer teamwork among students, the promotion of active learning, the delivering of timely and helpful feedback, and the communication of high expectations tend to yield strong academic results.[40]

In looking at social presence, Whiteside introduced the social presence model, which suggests that social presence consists of the elements: affective association, community cohesion, instructor involvement, interaction intensity, and knowledge and experience.[41] This list represents an exhaustive observation of teacher-student social interaction.

Teacher interaction and involvement weigh heavily into the idea of social presence and the establishment of continuous teacher-student relationships. For virtual teaching to be as effective as possible, students need to view the teacher's presence as consistent, optimistic, kind, competent, thoughtful, and steady. If the student feels that the teacher truly cares about their success, that student will tend to perform better academically. Thus, teachers need to be engaged with, caring for, and visible to their students throughout the learning journey as they collaborate.

I recently presented during a professional development to the middle school faculty of the Violetta Virtual Academies. During that presentation, I asked the teachers who teach in virtual settings which they believed to be more important in building meaningful and productive teacher-student relationships and in fostering student academic success, teacher academic presence or teacher social presence. A tally of responses found that 95% of teachers stated that teacher social presence was more important than academic presence, with 5% stating that the two were equally important, and no one stating that academic presence alone was most important. These are real responses from teachers in the trenches.

Ultimately, a great effort placed on teacher presence, especially social, is vital to effectual virtual teaching, as student success often depends on the reduction of the transactional distance that exists between teacher and student. Instructor presence does considerably impact both student success and satisfaction. Teachers in virtual environments may build effective teacher-student relationships by paying special attention to planning for interaction, by setting clear expectations, and by allowing for opportunities for engagement. When a virtual teacher is mindful of the special circumstances surrounding the teacher-student relationship, especially in a virtual classroom, much can be done to bridge the gap that exists.

The ways in which teacher presence is approached in a virtual environment differ greatly from those of a brick-and-mortar classroom. To be truly effective, teacher planning needs to be always mindful of presence, as the virtual classroom knows a greater transactional distance between teacher and student than does the brink-and-mortar environment. Student success also depends on the degree to which teachers involved in virtual instruction are cognizant of the ways in which students perceive their teaching presence.[42]

Ultimately, teacher presence significantly impacts both academic success and student satisfaction. Teachers in virtual environments may build effective teacher-student relationships by focusing on interaction, setting clear expectations, nurturing student sense of belonging, and allowing for opportunities for engagement, both social and academic. Teacher presence is a key element to the teacher-student relationship, and special attention needs to be paid to overcoming the challenges of transactional distance in a virtual classroom. When a teacher who teaches virtually is mindful of the special circumstances on which the construction of, and productivity of, the teacher-student relationship depend, much can be done to bridge the gap that exists.

Social presence centers on the concept of nonacademic human interaction between the teacher and the students. Teacher presence needs to be consistent but not intimidating, as students find ways of hiding from uncomfortable interactions in virtual environments. In many cases, the academic success of the students was found to be tied to the teacher's social presence, as students who care about the teacher were found to try harder to succeed academically, hoping to not disappoint the teacher.

In line with the concept of teachers and students viewing one another as a human, and not just voices in an online lesson, is the idea that student sense of belonging is contingent on the safety felt by the students in the virtual classroom. When students feel welcome and comfortable, they are free to succeed.

DELIBERATE TEACHER PRESENCE

Teacher presence is a crucial piece of student learning, as it encompasses the ways in which a teacher piques student interest and stimulates intellectual curiosity. Of the themes revealed in this study, teacher presence was the theme most mentioned. Responses from all participants touched on the importance of deliberate teacher presence as being both planned and spontaneous. Each participant discussed specific classroom techniques that have been commonly used in the virtual environment to confirm teacher presence to better serve both the virtual student and the teacher themself.

TEACHER DISCUSSION ON SOCIAL PRESENCE

The responses from the participants in this study pointed to the idea that teacher social presence is a key factor in student academic success. Teacher social presence involves all nonacademic teacher-student interaction. Each of the eight participants in this study repeatedly mentioned human social interaction with students as a significant piece of student success. A cross sectional analysis of the transcripts of this study shows that teachers believe that building a strong teacher-student relationship involves the personal touch. This individual bond often translates to student academic achievement. Along these lines, Joy stated:

> So often we call them students and they just kind of become numbers. But respecting them as individuals I think is a big piece of that. For example, I've had a couple of students tell me: "This is how I'm feeling or this is what I'm going through. Please don't share this with my parents." And you have to make a determination, is it in their best interest for me to keep it quiet? And if it is, if it's not something that violates any policies, then I can do that and I can say: "Look, I respect what you're going through. This is you emerging into a whole person and you're on this path of joining society as a functioning member, so we want to make sure that you have the tools for that."

Clearly, what Joy is describing has little to do with academics and everything to do with seeing the student as a whole person. Joy has also found that this human connection is beneficial to the students in both a personal and an academic manner. In line with this thought process, Jill discussed the benefits of human interaction with students. She shared:

> I really appreciated how much I am able to spend individualized time with my students cultivating not only a true understanding of who they are, but what their family dynamic is, what their experiences are, where they struggle, how they function differently.

Further, Jill stated:

> I remember things, I write little notes to them throughout the school year and mail them out. Those extra details outside of [class], to build those human-to-human affections. I'll let them grab a camera and show me their new puppy . . . where the interest isn't just: "did you do my math quiz?" Or: "did you read? Did you finish your essay?" But really who they are.

Jill believes that the path to student success is the building of meaningful teacher-student relationships in the virtual environment. Mike shared a similar view when he stated:

> Sometimes it's just chatting with the students before and after class. It's paying attention to their likes and dislikes, engaging with them either through a microphone or through video cam. Sometimes it was just spending time after class letting the students draw or just talk about their day, let them engage with each other as well.

The act of getting to the core of the student as a person shows that the teacher cares. This theme of building a meaningful teacher-student relationship was mentioned by every participant. Again, we see social presence emerging as important to the nurturing of both the whole child and the student. Bobbie also described the human connection. She felt that the establishment of this connection was crucial to student self-esteem as well as student academic success. Bobbi shared:

> I'm going to get to know every single one of these kids. I want them to get to know me, and I want them to get to know each other. In eighth grade, that can be more of a challenge because obviously they want to share all kinds of things that I don't want them to share, but that's my number one goal.

When VIVA teachers begin the school year, connection calls are made to each student and parent/guardian. Then, throughout the year, enduring connections are made between the teacher and students. These connections often extend to other family members of the student. This call is a mandatory task for all VIVA teachers. Bobbi shared that her connection calls often take a long time. She stated that this is a good thing, as she starts each year knowing the obstacles the students are up against as well as student strengths. To Bobbi, getting a clear picture of each student is essential to being able to teach effectively.

Karen also shared her experiences with getting to know the students in her classroom personally. She stated:

> I try my best to kind of get to know students, the ones that are willing to open up to me, so that's number one. It's a little bit more difficult than in brick and mortar because students have a choice more so than in a brick and mortar whether they're going to talk to me or tell me anything really at all. . . . students that are more willing to share more about them, you're able to build relationships with them that are very similar to those that are in brick and mortar because they're willing to open up to you. Most of the time that I see this is students that maybe they don't have their parents around during the day, so they might be a little bit lonely almost, so they're willing to kind of give you more because they're getting attention and they're being able to talk to somebody, and they're not feeling as isolated. Because being online, I think everybody knows that you can feel a little bit isolated at times.

Karen's points of middle school student isolation and loneliness are well-taken, as socialization is a vital part of adolescence. As students are sometimes left alone at home, the responsibility of the teacher to create opportunities for the building of teacher-student, as well as student-student, relationships is critical.

Further, Karen commented that the students who are left alone at home are those whom she finds to be readily eager to connect with her and with their fellow students. Karen commented that she is: "able to have more robust conversations about things that they're into," than she can the students who are well supported at home. In terms of student-student relationships, Karen stated that she encourages students to talk outside of class, more so than in class, as she feels this allows for kids to be kids.

In this regard, personally, I have found that one of two realities is true. Either students who are left home alone will become very close to the teacher, or they will realize that they can hide and never participate, most likely doing something else during a live class. These students most need a teacher's social presence.

Daisy also talked a great deal about getting to know the students personally. Going a step further, she focused on the concept of the teacher working to establish the idea to the students that they actually want to be there teaching them. This is powerful. She emphasized this point on teacher engagement with these statements:

> Basically, just making them feel like you want to be there, not like it's just another day at work, making them feel like you're enthusiastic about what you're doing. That's good teacher presence, making them know that you're there for them, reminding them that you're there for them. . . . if they have respect for you and know that you respect them and you want them to do well in school, they're going to work harder for you and they're going to ask you for help if they don't know, is my motto. It's not the same for every student obviously, but that's kind of a general trend is my thought.

At VIVA, each student is required to have a supervising adult at home. These managers are known as *learning coaches*. The learning coach typically works with the student on most aspects of school, including course content, ensuring the student's attendance, being present at teacher conferences, and helping the student with the creation of a daily schedule.

Learning coaches are a vital part of the equation in determining student success in the virtual classroom. This also ties in with the idea of a student's community of inquiry. Making a strong connection with the student's educational stakeholders is important in understanding a given student's home situation. Daisy discussed her dynamic with learning coaches in terms of social presence and student engagement.

> You have to build that rapport with the families and whatever it takes to build that rapport. You have to build the rapport with the learning coach, not just the students, but the learning coach as well. So, the learning coach trusts you and trusts that their child, whatever, is in good hands. So, you have to do that. I'll be on the phone sometimes with these families for, it's ridiculous, for like forty-five minutes because it's not just all business all the time.

Continuing, Daisy stated:

> Anyway, I want to know how so-and-so's doing after recovering from COVID, something like that. It's just like, you have to take notes on all this stuff and their families and try to respond as much as I can and follow up with things with them so that they know I'm not just here just as a teacher. I'm also here to support you with whatever I need to support you with. Sometimes I don't always have time to do as much as I would like to do, but again, we can't be everybody's best friend, but we just need to make sure that they know that we're here for them.

Michelle's story shares similarities with Daisy's, in terms of building rapport with both students and learning coaches. In discussing the establishment of social presence as a part of her daily routine in ensuring a solid teacher-student relationship, Michelle stated:

> For me, they're able to talk to me before and after class about whatever they want. Homeroom for me, I think, is really kind of low key. I give them the announcements, stuff I want them to know, which typically only takes five or ten minutes. Then, the rest of the time is theirs. We play games or just hang out type of thing. I've found that students are more willing to engage in class or even say: "Hey, I have a question. I need help," if they know that the teacher actually really cares and is really interested in what they have to say, whether big, little, important or not. So, I would typically, and for virtual especially, I don't see my students face to face. The cameras are on during class, but in brick and mortar they're all right there typically, not in a pandemic year. So being able to, so building this relationship, especially from day one is vital and important.

Michelle's experience of allowing students the opportunity for taking time to get to know one another, as well as the teacher, as people and not just voices on the microphone and faces on a screen was mentioned by all of this study's participants as crucial to student success in the virtual environment. To students, the virtual environment can get lonely and feel isolating at times. It is the responsibility of the teacher to facilitate these opportunities to allow students and learning coaches to socialize. Although teacher social presence is hugely important, so then is academic teacher presence.

TEACHER ACADEMIC PRESENCE

Although all teaching is multifaceted, teaching in the virtual environment involves a few unique challenges. As we have seen in the literature, teacher presence in terms of academics can be the deciding factor in student success. To teach concepts, model correct practices for lessons, and guide student group and independent work, a teacher must be present in the academics of a class. Academically, the teacher puts curriculum into action. As the educational classroom model of this research is virtual, as Mike stated: "It's definitely important for the student to have that person that they're responsible to." At the end of the day, assignments are due.

Joy

Joy used the analogy of a Sherpa in her description of good academic teacher presence, discussing the ways in which a teacher guides the students through what, at times, seems like mountains of work and responsibility. When discussing academic teacher presence, Joy shared:

We are like the Sherpa, we're the ones who know the path and we're supposed to be teaching them how to find it. On my signature on my email, I have that little quote that just says: "Education is not the learning of facts but the training of the mind to think," by Albert Einstein. That's the real key.

I don't care if you have to go outside of the school to find the information as long as you're not just straight plagiarizing and cheating. If you know how to search down that information, you're halfway to being a functional adult because nobody on the street is asking me to recite facts about distant wars. I would just Google that. But I'm trying to teach critical thinking skills and personal accountability more so than science facts or math facts.

Here, Joy discussed the importance of guided practice and offering students the opportunity to succeed in a real-world manner. She talked about guiding the students rather than teaching at them. This is a distinction that is clearly important to her. Along these lines, Joy continued:

I try I think with my students to say: "Hey, I'm totally here for you and I'm part of your team and we're going to get you to the finish line. But you're the one who really has to take the reins on this because otherwise we're just dragging you like a lump of coal across this finish line, and that's not where you want to be. You want to be in charge of your own destiny."

Joy's philosophy of guiding the students without babysitting them has worked well for her and has clearly communicated to the students that the fate of their academic success is ultimately in their hands.

Michelle

Michelle also discussed student engagement as it applies to lessons. To her, a major piece of academic success is setting expectations while offering positive reinforcement. She also found that: "the more that teachers are present, the more students succeed." In discussing her practice of ensuring student engagement, Michelle shared:

I keep encouraging. I remind of participation points and when they won't engage, then I call families to discuss the importance of engaging in the lesson . . . a lot of positive praise. Say I had Bobby here, who wasn't really engaged much, but I saw he raised his hand to read. I let him read and say: "Thank you very much. I really appreciate it." A lot of encouragement. A lot of positive reinforcement. For me, presence is kind of acknowledging what they're doing. Saying: "Hey, I see it. I appreciate what you're doing."

VIVA recently started using new software called Newrow. Newrow allows the teachers and students the ability to see and hear one another, as well as providing screen-sharing options that allow the teacher to utilize PowerPoint presentations, screen-share websites from the internet, and create quizzes for the students. In continuing to discuss the ways in which student participation and student engagement influence academics, as well as her own utilization of VIVA's new teaching software, Newrow, Michelle stated:

> I give weekly participation points. They have to attend and show that they are participating in some way. I discuss with student and families that, if it makes them more comfortable, the student can private chat me their questions and answers to my questions that I ask. That really helps my shy and anxiety prone students. I use the Newrow tools often and at random. This way students don't go on autopilot and they have to pay attention to what tool I have them use and when.

Michelle identified a great deal of her teacher presence with her results regarding participation and student engagement. By offering the option of privately chatting their responses to her, she made special allowances for students who were uncomfortable talking on the microphone. In this way, Michelle could assert her presence and check for student engagement without making the student feel uncomfortable. This approach is similar to that of Jill's. Jill stated:

> I have a few kids who really struggle with sharing out their thinking in the whole group setting, will private message me out. I'll say: "A student said this, what are your thoughts?" Because they're still a part of that learning process, but it's really encouraging them to build the interaction. And when they can [interact], it needs, I don't want to say pushing, but guiding them along through that process because it's very easy for our kids to be, what they call the passive learner. Right?

Daisy

Daisy talked about effective teacher presence in terms of fostering engagement and participating. In discussing her approach to class, she stated that her outward manner and attitude were paramount to student engagement. She shared:

> Being on time, being happy, having a joyful, I don't know how to say it, but you know what I mean? Not being monotone, like having a happy tone ... making it seem like it's exciting to be in there instead of just like: "Yeah, good morning."

Daisy's philosophy reaches back into teacher social presence by showing the students that she is there for them and truly cares. In asserting her teacher presence, Daisy took a hands-on approach with a specific lesson she discussed during the interview. Each year, as part of a geology unit, sixth grade VIVA students identify rocks and characteristics of rocks in rock kits. A rock presentation is the capstone project for that unit. Daisy discussed that lesson in terms of her constructive academic teacher presence. She stated:

> So, when we were doing the rock presentation for science, and it really helps for them to use manipulatives while you are teaching. So, it was really cool because I had them break out their rock kits that they all have when we were going through rocks. So, I put them in the breakout rooms. I think I'd put this in the Skype too, but it was a great lesson. . . . they were all totally into it because they were looking at all their rocks and they were talking to each other and because they had those manipulatives, they had something there, like a tangible thing that they could look at and do. So that worked out really well.

Daisy's use of Zoom and manipulatives allowed her to guide the practice while still keeping her lesson student-centered. She facilitated learning by granting students the opportunity to see one another while guiding their discussion to that of the rocks.

Like Michelle, Daisy's teacher academic presence places importance on positive reinforcement and not on the negative. She stated that this approach fosters student engagement. Daisy described her approach in these terms.

> We're talking constantly and, what am I trying to say? We're checking for understanding constantly. They know that when they are entering their answers, I only respond positively. I don't say: "Jack, that was incorrect. Do that again." It's positive reinforcement when they do get it correct. So that helps them to know: "Okay . . ." I try to encourage by positive encouragement if, that makes sense. But I don't discourage by saying that that is wrong. What I do tell them is if you do not hear me call your name, you need to rethink your answer. So, they know that I'm constantly monitoring the answers that they're putting in and monitoring when they're putting in the chat.

This idea of creating a safe space for students to get a question either right or wrong without being ridiculed is important and was a repeated theme throughout this study. When a student is shot down quickly, they often tune out and get nothing from the lesson. Harshly dismissing a student's wrong answer also dissuades that student from future participation. Continuing, Daisy discussed her presence in terms of keeping students on track. She shared the following.

> So, I'll tell them, I'll say: "That doesn't look like that's an appropriate thing that we should be talking about. Let's stay focused." Just making sure that they know that I am there, and I am monitoring everything that they're doing.

Daisy is quite involved in her classes while maintaining the trust of the students and allowing for student-centered learning. She utilizes cameras, chat, private chat, and breakout rooms to be present while allowing students opportunities to establish their own presence.

Much like Daisy, Tammy relies a great deal on preplanned student activities that emphasize visuals and human interaction. She repeatedly stressed the importance of her students being on camera. For her, the ability to see her students on screen is a vital piece of each student lesson, as well as student academic success. In discussing her own academic teacher presence, Tammy stated:

> Well, first and foremost, [what is important is] encouraging everyone to turn their cameras on, because the visuals really help. And I can see facial expressions and things like that. Also, regular phone calls, I have a lot of open sessions where I invite the learning coaches. And all those things, together, help. And then there's our student connection calls, which I'm finding of late I get more responses on those if I text instead of call. Having my camera on, having a good sense of humor, but also being very clear with them, sending very clear communication. "What are our goals? What are we going to be learning about today? What do I expect from you?" So, it's clear communication, but also being human.

The communication of clear expectations to students is always crucial to their learning. In a virtual classroom, however, it can be a challenge to ensure that the expectations were received by a student. Tammy shared that the visual of seeing a student on camera, seeing the student's reactions and body language, and getting a verbal confirmation helps to confirm the conveyance of communication. On this point, Tammy shared:

> Well, the way I've discussed it, both with learning coaches and parents, we need to be looking at each other. Suppose we were on the street or in my regular classroom talking, you wouldn't put a cover over your head while we're talking, right? There would be both a visual and an auditory exchange.

Tammy discussed the ways in which her teacher presence helps to foster student engagement and, further, how that process translates to actual student academic success. She stated that she can see a direct positive correlation between on camera student engagement and student success. Tammy stated:

> The more I'm engaged, the more they're engaged, and that's something I really believe fundamentally. The more they see me and understand where I'm coming from by seeing my face, hearing my voice, I think it increases their engagement as well. I see more assignments being turned in. I see more questions asked; and

as long as they know what I look like and I'm not just the voice in the sky, it definitely helps. I try to do extra things with them, too.

I'll open up a study group time where they can all study with each other; and I try to think out of the box a little bit and have them do things like a study group where they can all work together on a project, or just a time when they can just sit and talk to each other. And those things have helped, tremendously.

Overall, Tammy has great confidence in seeing the students on camera. She explained her reasons for her pro-camera claim through her experience in observing greater student engagement, which leads to better academic success, when students are interacting on camera. This interaction also hearkens back to the importance of social presence. Tammy's teacher academic presence is found in her planning, which is underscored with both deliberate teacher academic and social presence.

Karen

Unlike Tammy, Karen did not talk much about the use of student cameras. However, she did make a connection between her presence and student engagement. Her recipe for strong student engagement and the building of meaningful and productive teacher-student relationships is in her consistent interactions with students. Karen shared:

Effective teacher presence in an online environment kind of just looks like, first of all, you're responding constantly either to the group through chat, through a microphone, or you're doing it privately through private chat; and a lot of times, I will let students know, if there's dead air during class, something like: "Oh, I'm just responding to somebody really quick and we're going to move on after this," so that they actually know what it is that I'm doing at all times.

They hear my voice a lot, they see me typing in chat a lot, they see me using whiteboard tools a lot. . . . unless my computer freezes, they can expect to see something come up in chat, hear my voice, or there's something going on at the board at all times.

Unlike some of the other teachers interviewed, Karen pushed back on the idea that teacher presence is a key learning tool for all students. She stated that although there are definitely groups of students who benefit from deliberate teacher academic presence, not all students benefit from having a responsive teacher. Karen broke this phenomenon down into three groups of students. She shared:

In general, I'd say that there is a correlation between student success and teacher presence. However, I know that there are some students that are going to be successful regardless of the teacher presence and it doesn't matter what I do. They're still going to be successful. For kind of like the middle group of students, I'd say that the teacher presence does make a big difference. Because for students of the age that I'm working with, it's very easy for them to be like, "Oh, well, nobody really cares. Nobody is really watching what I'm doing." Or "she doesn't really know what I'm up to."

And so, it is important for those students to know that I do know what they're doing, and I can see what they're doing every day, and that I am monitoring things that they're saying in the chat, not just to me but to other people, as well. So, I'd say that there's always going to be different groups of students, those that need more of a teacher presence to stay motivated, and some that don't need it; and then there's also that third group of students where no matter how overbearing my presence is, they're just going to keep ignoring it. So, there's always going to be three baskets of students there.

Karen's dissection of student engagement is similar to what Mike mentioned on the same issue. He shared:

What motivates one student may not motivate another. I try to think of what this environment would look like if there was no teacher attached to it if they did it all on their own. You'd have a wide variety of students who could possibly be extremely successful in that, but then you'd also have the flip side where there'd be students that would not thrive. They would not advance in that environment.

Although Karen's and Mike's analysis of teacher-led student engagement addresses the real issue of individualized needs for individual students, Bobbi's academic teacher presence connects accountability and follow-through with student engagement. Bobbi intertwines social presence with academic presence to confirm student engagement. She shared:

I have a checklist of every single kid, and did they do this? Did they do this? And, did they do this? That data, I do scrutinize because I feel like I can tell ... who's not engaged. They're minimally checking the boxes or they're minimally coming to class, but they're not actively engaged. I've learned that, and I think that's a critical piece of success, and just over-communication versus under-communication. Conferences, phone calls, emails.

Bobbi

Bobbi stressed communication and personal attention toward students as methods of nurturing student engagement and, ultimately, student success. Again, we see a great deal of the focus placed on social presence. Bobbi discussed the ways in which she allows for her social presence to complement her academic presence when she stated:

Just staying in touch and having them know there's a teacher on the other end of the phone and I care about their well-being, number one, and their academic success, number two, and sometimes academic success is first. They have to do it.

As Bobbi utilizes a combination, in seemingly equal parts, of social presence and academic presence, she refuses to embarrass students who are actively participating. She will, however, call out students who are disengaged. Bobbi shared:

I actively mention in conferences that I do NOT call out kids who are paying attention, but I DO call out those who I think are not paying attention. I will text parents during sessions, send post-session attendance emails, mention it in IEP meetings and/or conferences.

This kind of follow-through really helps Bobbi stay on top of student engagement in her classroom.

Jill

Similar to Bobbi's approach, Jill discussed her teacher academic presence as a combination of social and academic, always planned, with an eye on making personal connections, while identifying the need for a spontaneous shift in strategy if needed. Jill discussed her warm-up activities as such:

When I come into class, I always have a warm-up on the board. I have a timer on for kids to know exactly when we're going to get started, and I do that every class period every day. I'm talking to the kids, checking in. I tell them, I'm turning my mic off, private chat on, this is the time to ask questions. They know that. So, they know when is the appropriate time to communicate things because sometimes the kids want to do that.

Jill continued, discussing her ongoing attempts to reach all students through her academic teacher presence. She shared a certain frustration in being unable to get 100% participation from her students. She also discussed students who do too much in a group setting, allowing the other students to become spectators in class. Jill shared:

I feel like I'm flying. I'm putting as many tricks in things that I can find to get them to communicate with me while I'm in the classes. Right? How long do you wait for students to respond before moving on? How many different ways do you have? I found it more successful though, I'm still not 100%. . . . instead of doing two problems in a class period that we practiced together, we're doing one, but we're breaking it down in steps, or having kids to read out loud or answering question getting them to participate and writing on the whiteboard.

But then there's always one student who's doing all of the chores of the other kids. That seems to be where I struggle the most because they don't know how to balance. We have to get out of the box clearly, but it's like, do I kick them out? When do I kick? How often do I need to follow up? That's where I struggle because when there's disengagement, you're playing the guessing games, and especially because these are the same students whose parents are disengaged.

Jill's struggles are not unique, as some of the other participants shared similar frustrations. Still, when academic presence is obvious, those students who need and will accept assistance will ultimately get the help they need. Also, bringing the student's family into the equation is key here. Like Jill, I have also found that students who disengage typically have parents who are disengaged. This is where I usually find myself texting the family. It seems that, these days, many families are truly much more likely to respond to a text than to an email.

WHEN IS TEACHER PRESENCE SPONTANEOUS AND WHEN IS IT PLANNED?

In analyzing teacher use of presence in the middle school virtual classroom, this study asked the participants to discuss whether teacher presence was mostly planned or mostly spontaneous. Each participant stated that for teacher presence to be effective in the virtual environment, the planning of presence was necessary, but the recognition of and acting upon the opportunity for spontaneity was also essential. For instance, Jill stated that while she always "maps things out," the need for flexibility is a must. She shared that she often stops during class to check for student understanding. If there is a noticeable lack of student understanding, she "scraps" her planned approach and addresses the class from a different angle. Similarly, Tammy shared that in her experience, both planned and spontaneous teacher presence had been necessary for effective teaching in the virtual environment.

Further, Tammy communicated that, during planning, she would write prompts into her lesson plans that would serve as cues to remind her to pause herself, to ask questions, or to open a class discussion. These self-prompts have been necessary. However, she acknowledged the reality of being in the moment and the spontaneity that can keep a lesson alive when it is in danger of failing.

To this point, Joy discussed the need to "read the room." She also stated that it is important to feel the moment, as spontaneity is often a necessary component of teacher presence. Likewise, Daisy discussed the realities of seasoning her preplanned presence with spontaneity, stating that sometimes,

"I just pull something out of my hat." She went on to say: "we've got to have a plan, but we also divert from our plans all the time as we go along."

Like the other participants, Daisy has found it necessary to adjust the approach of her presence as needed. Similarly, Mike stated that his presence is typically "all planned," but: "the spontaneous part of it is just reacting and engaging with the student." Only Michelle and Karen shared that their teaching presence is mainly spontaneous.

Each teacher shared that years ago, as new to teaching virtually, they would spend more time planning for teacher presence. However, while they utilize both spontaneous and planned presence, both Michelle and Karen stated that they now use spontaneity more often than they do planned teaching presence. Clearly, teacher presence is on the minds of each of these middle school teachers in virtual settings. They each recognized the fact that lessons can change, necessitating a differing approach to teaching. Planning for presence, such as writing cues into the lesson plans works well for some of the teachers, while identifying the need for spontaneity helps all teachers from time to time.

Whether spontaneous or planned, teacher presence has been found to be a crucial element in the success of middle school students learning virtually. While planning for teacher presence is key to student success, spontaneity is an important tool to possess, as lessons do not always go as planned. The participants of this study utilize both planned and spontaneous teacher presence as needed. Personally, I plan for presence and then adjust, as needed.

THOUGHTS ON ENGAGEMENT

Each of the participants in this study has an approach that places student engagement in a position of great importance. Although this engagement is attained through various means and methods, teacher academic presence is a key ingredient in the overall academic success of the students. As mentioned, some students will succeed with or without a teacher. Other students will simply ignore a teacher with even the strongest presence. However, many students rely on teacher academic presence to introduce them to and guide them through opportunities for academic success. There are varied ways a teacher may be present for academics, but in the end, student engagement and, ultimately, student academic success will be determined by the output of the student. The nurturing of the opportunities for this output is a major piece of what makes for an effective virtual middle school teacher. When a student feels supported in this manner and recognizes the classroom as a safe space, the chances for building a meaningful and productive teacher-student relationship are strengthened.

STUDENT SAFETY

Safety in the virtual middle school environment often means that a student feels comfortable enough with a teacher to participate or at least engage on some level with the teacher, as well as with the content, without fear of unnecessary backlash or mockery. This type of classroom safety is freeing in that it has the potential to unlock a student's innermost ability, relegating insecurities to the background and allowing for unconstrained learning.

Throughout the series of interviews for this study, the concept of student safety emerged as a common thread that could not be ignored. Without fail, every teacher in this study described the establishment of student safety in the classroom as an absolute requirement for the building of meaningful and productive teacher-student relationships. The teachers also viewed safety as essential for student success. The fostering of a safe space is key to the building of strong and meaningful teacher-student relationships. Daisy discussed student safety as an integral part of her daily teaching, sharing the ways in which it encourages student engagement.

> So, I think it's just the safety thing is huge and it gets them to participate more if they know they're not afraid to come to class, they know that it's a safe environment and just knowing that you're there for them. I mean, you have to build a relationship with these kids, otherwise they're not going to want to participate at all, or they're not going to want to come to class.

In discussing student confidence in a safe classroom environment, Daisy stated:

> I always remind them if it does not make sense, there's no judgment in here. You have to tell me if it doesn't make sense and then we'll work on it together. I get a lot of kids that tell me it doesn't make sense. They're not embarrassed to say, to give the sad face. I like that too. They feel comfortable in there.

Daisy's example is representative of the comments given by each participant as they discussed student safety in the classroom. The idea that students are comfortable answering a question or completing a math problem without fear of judgment from either the teacher or the other students is, indeed, hugely beneficial to the atmosphere of learning. In correlating a safe classroom environment with the building of strong teacher-student relationships, Daisy stated:

> Well, I think that the closer the relationship you have with your students, the harder they're going to try for you. They're also going to feel safer to reach out to you if they don't understand. So, if they're afraid to come to you for help,

then you haven't established a good relationship with them . . . you just have to make sure that they know it's a safe environment.

Daisy designated the establishment of safety in the virtual classroom as necessary to the building of strong teacher-student relationships and in nurturing academic success. Daisy's examples from the classroom linked safety with student success rates.

Likewise, Michelle has discovered that student safety is significant in the trust that is built between teachers and students. She also intertwined social presence and her own introversion into the equation. Michelle stated:

> Students, typically they want to see that the teacher cares about them. They want to see that the teacher is there and going to help them. . . . for me, just learning boundaries and going: "Okay." I've always been pretty good at creating a warm environment and making kids feel safe and wanted, but for me it was more about finding boundaries and figuring out what works for me and how good I could be with me being as introverted as I am. Took a couple years trying to figure it out.

While Michelle touched on the idea that, for success to be realized, students need to know that a teacher cares and provides a warm environment, Joy took safety a step further, characterizing her learning space as a safety zone and describing herself as the students' "second mom." Stating that she has "a mom heart" and that her "mom heart feels for them." Joy shared:

> I really feel that it's necessary to go out of your way to provide that safe space for students, and it's really challenging in a virtual environment, it so is, that you just have to keep reminding them that you care. . . . I think students really have to know that you care; that you are not just here doing a job and that you need them to work so that people are off your back. They need to know that you really invest in them and care about them personally. So, that means putting your own stuff aside and focusing on what's important to them.

Here, Joy's "mom heart" was on full display, as she repeatedly stated that the students have to know that the teacher cares. Her practice of putting her own personal issues aside for the good of the student has allowed her to build strong and meaningful teacher-student relationships. For Joy, part of this relationship is seeing the student as a person and not just a name on her roster. She did not shy away from the realities of life experience when she stated:

> Treating the whole student is the only way to access the things they care about because they're not going to tell you in the middle of a math thing that their mom committed suicide a year ago and they're really struggling with that. They're going to tell you that in a private chat during a share time when you're

being vulnerable, and they feel like they have access to you and that you invest in them.

Jill also described her students as "my children." Her approach also comes from a whole-child perspective that values growth over immediate feedback. She shared:

> So, I really, as an educator firmly believe in cultivating a safe learning environment. I really consider my students my children. They are mine because I get to walk through a year of their learning, which is a part of their growth and development. I feel unlike when I taught in brick-and-mortar, I have the opportunities, maybe not as much as I like it under our current parameters, just because of the restrictions, but in all my years, I really appreciated how much I am able to spend individualized time with my students cultivating not only a true understanding of who they are, but what their family dynamic is, what their experiences are, where they struggle, how they function differently.
>
> We are consistent. You can count on me. You don't get out of doing these things, but I will provide you as much support as you need in those processes. So, when things happen or when mistakes are made, it's safe. I always tell the kids it's safe to make mistakes with me. It's safe to be real with me. I hear you.

Again, Joy and Jill each delved deep into their experience to discuss a strong commitment to student safety, viewing the child as a person, as well as sharing the dividends this approach has paid in terms of teacher-student relationships. Social presence was on full display in their remarks. Correspondingly, Mike shared his thoughts on the importance of student safety, discussing student understanding of the safe learning space he has provided. He stated:

> Just, I think it has a lot to do with students understanding what's okay, what's not okay. Understanding that they're in a safe environment where they're not going to be bullied or made fun of, where they feel that they can express themselves even if they're wrong. I think that's the goal.

Mike also shared that while not all students are comfortable getting an answer wrong and are, thus, afraid to participate in the live sessions, many students have no problem with being corrected in his safe space. Fearless student attitudes, such as these are a testament to the teacher-student relationships that he has been able to cultivate. Mike shared:

> I think when students feel comfortable participating, even though they lack the skill, that shows me that not only are they willing to learn, but they're willing to try. . . . I have a lot of students who don't want to participate in a group because they're afraid that they're going to get an answer wrong. But then, on the flip

side, I have students who will try, and even though they get it wrong, they welcome the correction.

You see the correction, and you see them move forward with that correction. Those are the ones that I consider good things. . . . The ones that engage in the classroom, that they're active, they're responding, those are the ones that you know that they feel comfortable, that they're happy, especially if it's focused on the lesson at hand.

Mike's safe space has allowed for this engagement and for the building of teacher-student relationships, as the students feel safe in the virtual learning space.

In line with the common thread of recognizing safety as a priority, Bobbi discussed the need for safety and described her virtual classroom as a family of sorts. For her, a great deal of the student safety she fosters comes in the form of fun, team-building and social activities. Bobbi shared:

> I think safety is number one. I want every student in my classroom, and we talk about it a lot. . . . First of all, we do homeroom every day. Our pod, I work in a pod of three, we do homeroom five days a week . . . we do birthdays and we do trivia and we do the weekly plan, and we have Q&A sessions and if you did some awesome artwork, you can send it in, or if you've got a cute pet, you send it in, or if you juggle, we'll put you on camera. So, this number one rule is we are an eighth-grade family. We support each other.

Continuing, Bobbi stated that the students: "need a safety net and the safety net has to be the teacher." She views her role in this community as that of facilitator of the safe space, as she utilizes her social presence to create a comfortable and safe environment.

THOUGHTS ON SAFETY

Each participant viewed student safety as a crucial component to student success in the virtual environment. Feeling comfortable to raise one's hand and possibly get an answer wrong without fear of reprimand or ridicule is key to a student's comfort. When a student finds this comfort on a level that allows for unreserved participation, it is freeing. Ultimately, this identification of safety allows a student the freedom to succeed.

Many of the participants identified themselves as a sort of parental figure in the classroom. From allowing students to text them at all hours of the night, to talking on the phone and private chatting with the students, these teachers see their role as more than that of a teacher who works from 8:30 to 4:00,

Monday to Friday. These teachers are giving, caring people who work to identify the needs and special circumstances of their students.

It is in the sincerity of these gestures and practices that the students find the safety they need to succeed. It is true that not all teachers are as accommodating with their time as are the participants in this study. However, the safety practices discussed in this study have been found to be effective. When the teacher is real and human with the students, the students usually respond positively. Thus, the teacher-student relationship has been reinforced. Student safety in the virtual environment is necessary if a teacher is to nurture student sense of belonging.

DELIBERATE TEACHER PRESENCE IS NECESSARY IN THE VIRTUAL ENVIRONMENT

Each participant in this study told stories in which teaching presence, especially social, was linked to student engagement and, ultimately, found to be crucial to student academic success. Six of the eight participants shared that their teaching presence was planned. Although spontaneous teaching presence was discussed by all participants as a necessity when teaching in any environment, the act of deliberately planning for teaching presence was considered to be necessary to those six teachers. The other two teachers who stated that their presence was mostly spontaneous shared that they had previously planned for presence but, after gaining experience in the virtual environment, had decided to rely on instinct for presence. Even in the two cases when teaching presence was mostly considered to be spontaneous, the importance of strong teaching presence was agreed to be key to student success. Garrison et al. shared that the formation of student cognitive presence and social presence tended to depend fundamentally on the presence of a teacher.[43]

Similarly, but in specifically considering virtual classroom environments, it is important to note that student success does indeed depend on the degree to which teachers involved in virtual instruction are cognizant of the ways in which students perceive their teaching presence. Thus, a teacher's cognizance of their own teaching presence can go a long way in fostering academic student success and development of the whole child.

Ultimately the stories told in this study backed the notion that teaching presence is that moment in which a teacher piques student interest and stimulates intellectual curiosity. Further, teaching presence allows the opportunity for student sense of belong to be formed. Effective teacher presence also helps to establish a safe space for students to participate without fear of unnecessary criticism and mockery.

The participants in this study acknowledged that the virtual environment can be isolating to the students. The responsibility of filling this void falls to the teacher to assert academic and social presence, while fostering and allowing for opportunities for teacher-student and student-student interaction.

To truly build meaningful and productive relationships with students, middle school teachers who teach virtually need to make teacher presence a priority. Teacher social presence should be recognized and respected as a vital element in virtual student academic success. As discussed by the participants in this study, when teachers get to know the students personally and when the students get to know the teacher as a human and not just as an authority figure, students do tend to perform better academically. To put it bluntly, students will often try harder for a teacher they like. Social presence, then, is key to building not only teacher-student relationships but also to fostering student academic success. Teacher presence should be included in the lesson plans of the middle school teacher who teaches in a virtual setting, as this planning will not only grant social presence the respected place it deserves in planning but will also serve as a reminder to the teacher to be socially and academically present.

THE STUDENT AS A NUANCED INDIVIDUAL

This study revealed that a great deal of effective teacher presence has much to do with creating a human connection with students and less to do with academics. The participants shared stories of planning virtual birthday celebrations, allowing students to call and text them at all hours, driving great distances to meet in-person with students, chatting with students during class, and paying specific attention to their personal likes and dislikes.

Ultimately, teaching presence was found to be at its most effective when teachers viewed their students as nuanced individuals, got to know them personally, and, in one way or another, became involved in their lives, outside of the academic setting and without the usual undertones of academic expectation found in any given teacher-student relationship. These deliberate social actions align with Dewey, who shared that education is a "social process."

Although the teacher-student interactions described by the participants in this study were not always academic in nature, the academic success of those students actively involved in the social activities did, in fact, improve, as did student engagement. Aligning with this concept, the idea that teaching presence has predicted both student satisfaction and academic achievement supports teacher feedback. In discussing the teacher's need to connect with not only the academic student but also with the nuanced individual, research has found that middle schoolers often display a strong need for support and approval from peers and adults, whether or not they admit it.[44] Similarly, evidence suggests that when students were not validated by feedback from teachers, the result was a lowered sense of student academic engagement and enthusiasm. This lack of engagement produces lowered academic results.

Instructors involved in virtual instruction are better able to make connections when they pay close attention to the ways in which their teaching presence is realized by learners. Thus, teacher social presence when utilized to get to know students outside of an academic setting has proved to be beneficial to overall student success. Given the virtual nature and transactional distance of virtual schools, the teacher in a virtual setting must be especially deliberate in the formation and use of presence and in the nurturing of teacher-student relationships. Ultimately, deliberate teacher presence was found to be instrumental in the building of meaningful and productive teacher-student relationships.

The ways in which teacher presence is approached in a virtual environment differ greatly from those of a brick-and-mortar classroom. To be truly effective, teacher planning needs to be always mindful of presence, as the virtual classroom knows a greater transactional distance between teacher and student than does the brink-and-mortar environment. Student success also depends on the degree to which teachers involved in virtual instruction are cognizant of the ways in which students perceive their teaching presence.

Teacher presence significantly impacts both academic success and student satisfaction. Teachers in virtual environments may build effective teacher-student relationships by focusing on interaction, setting clear expectations, nurturing student sense of belonging, and allowing for opportunities for engagement, both social and academic. Teacher presence is a key element to the teacher-student relationship, and special attention needs to be paid to overcoming the challenges of transactional distance in a virtual classroom. When a teacher in a virtual setting is mindful of the special circumstances on which the construction of, and productivity of, the teacher-student relationship depend, much can be done to bridge the gap that exists.

In discussing teacher presence with the faculty and administration of our school, I asked for teacher input on presence. The following section is the transcript of that discussion. Again, names have been removed.

FROM THE PD!

How Do You Bring Teacher Presence to Your Classroom?

> Catch them being good!
> Social presence helps them stay engaged, especially with middle school.

even with little kids, social presence is essential
I welcome each student by name.
Our homeroom has a class mascot
Kids share out their favorites, songs, games, etc.
I send certificates and snail mail
I tell them it is not "MY" class, it is "OUR" class.
We have Show and tell
I have them share their interests
talent show
Rose and Thorn
Celebrate small successes
We are a team. . . . we are there to help and support each other.
don't start the recording during personal sharing
Ask about their week and weekend
Say hello to each one by name each day
I talk with them, like have actual conversations, share and listen to them.
Share myself and allow them to share
share about myself, personal
Ice breakers
Kids choose my background.
I welcome each student by name. Allow students to have classroom jobs.
I say each student's name EVERY session
I use student moderators
Virtual class pictures
Ask silly questions of the day. share "good things"
I try and give them opportunities to share their own points of view on things
acknowledgements of each other
hobby hangouts in HRCC
Kids are able to show off drawings, things they love . . . etc.
I give choices (where I can)
My students are literally part of my home. They tell my husband to quiet down, they welcome my children each morning before they go off to school.
telling them their thoughts and answers matter
Allow Sharing (music, art, etc.)
share their art
tell them how much they mean to me!
Remind them that we are a family
Compliments
Using their names, acknowledging them as they come in and answer or participate, share interest

Student kahoots about each kid

I love the rose and thorn. Using polling happy faces to see how they are doing that day. Follow up with any sad face students

Talk about ourselves, play games, breakout rooms, lessons on growth and confidence, remembering their interests

I take notes on each student so I can follow up on what's going on with them

Daily check ins, play music, send birthday cards

share their interests and incorporate into powerpoints and openers

Listening and remembering what they share about themselves, adding in personal information to my teaching

I tell them that I was a special ed student myself and I will tell them all of my techniques

Just started rose and thorn

Students are creating weekly new segments to lead the class

We do not correct each other. They love that one!

We also have a HR DJ who plays music at the end of class

HAVE FUN

Let students lead the class in homeroom

THOUGHTS ON PRESENCE

Through an exhaustive review of the literature and through my discussions with the participants of this study, I found that while the virtual middle school environment carries with it many challenges, those challenges can be met through proper planning and a respect for, and awareness of, the challenges of transactional distance known to the virtual middle school environment. In utilizing effective teacher presence, middle school teachers who teach virtually can create safe, comfortable, and productive virtual spaces for students to flourish.

This study also found that middle school teachers who teach virtually can find and have found effective ways to close the gap of transactional distance known to the virtual environment, often by utilizing social presence to appeal to the students on a human level. These social interactions often have little to do with academics but ultimately work to produce positive academic results. Through deliberate teacher presence and the actions that make up this presence middle school students truly can build meaningful and productive relationships with their teachers and peers in virtual environments.

In the virtual middle school classroom environment, productive teacher-student relationships are possible. Through effective use of teacher presence, teacher-student relationships can, and often do, foster student success. Our focus on transactional distance and teacher presence leads us to another important piece of the puzzle that is teacher-student relationships in the virtual classroom: students' sense of belonging.

NOTES

1. Peacock, S., & Cowan, J. (2019). Promoting sense of belonging in online learning communities of inquiry in accredited courses. *Online Learning, 23*(2), 67–81.
2. Purarjomandlangrudi, A., Chen, D., & Nguyen, A. (2016). Investigating the drivers of student interaction and engagement in online courses: A study of state-of-the-art. *Informatics in Education, 15*(2), 269–286.
3. Jackson, S. H. (2019). Student questions: A path to engagement and social presence in the online classroom. *Journal of Educators Online, 16*(1), 1–8.
4. Orcutt, J. M., & Dringus, L. P. (2017). Beyond being there: Practices that establish presence, engage students, and influence intellectual curiosity in structured online learning environment. *Online Learning, 21*(3), 15–35.
5. Umbach, P. D., & Wawrzynski, M. R. (2005). Faculty do matter: The role of college faculty in student learning and engagement. *Research in Higher Education, 46*(2), 153–184. https://doi.org/10.1007/s11162-004-1598-1
6. Oliphant, T., & Branch-Mueller, J. (2016). Developing a sense of community and the online student experience. *Education for Information, 32*(4), 307–321.
7. Kranzow, J. (2013). Faculty leadership in online education: Structuring courses to impact student satisfaction and persistence. *MERLOT Journal of Online Learning and Teaching, 9*(1), 131–139.
8. Eom, S. B., Wen, H. J., & Ashill, N. (2006). The determinants of students' perceived learning outcomes and satisfaction in university online education: An empirical investigation. Decision Sciences Journal of Innovative Education, 4(2), 215–235.
9. Mohd Khalid, M. N., & Quick, D. (2016). Teaching presence influencing online students' course satisfaction at an institution of higher education. *International Education Studies, 9*(3), 62–70.
10. Leese, M. (2009). Out of class—out of mind? The use of a virtual learning environment to encourage student engagement in out of class activities. *British Journal of Educational Technology, 40*(1), 70–77.
11. Anderson, T., Rourke, L. Garrison, R., & Archer, W (2001). Assessing teaching presence in a computer conferencing context. *Journal of Asynchronous Learning Networks, 5*(2), 1–17.
12. Garrison, D. R. (2000). Theoretical challenges for distance education in the 21st century: A shift from structural to transactional issues. *The International Review of Research in Open and Distributed Learning, 1*(1). https://doi.org/10.19173/irrodl.v1i1.2
13. Kucuk, S., & Richardson, J. C. (2019). A structural equation model of predictors of online learners' engagement and satisfaction. *Online Learning, 23*(2), 196–216.
14. Garrison, D. R., Anderson, T., & Archer, W. (2010). The first decade of the community of inquiry framework: A retrospective. *Internet and Higher Education, 13*(1–2), 5–9.

15. Dewey, J. (1933). *How we think*. Prometheus Books.

16. Dixson, M. D. (2010). Creating effective student engagement in online courses: What do students find engaging? *Journal of the Scholarship of Teaching and Learning, 10*(2), 1–13

17. Marks, R. B., Sibley, S. D., & Arbaugh, J. B. (2005). A structural equation model of predictors for effective online learning. *Journal of Management Education, 29*(10), 531–563.

18. Nishikant, S. (2009). The paradigm shift for adult education: From educational slavery to learning freedom of human brain with synaptic learning. In T. Kidd (Ed.), *Online education and adult learning: New frontiers for teaching practices* (pp. 150–164). IGI Global.

19. Ekmekci, O. (2013). Being there: Establishing presence in an online learning environment. *Higher Education Studies, 3*(1), 29–38. https://doi.org/10.5539/hes.v3n1p29

20. Akyol, Z., & Garrison, D. R. (2011). Assessing metacognition in an online community of inquiry. *The Internet and Higher Education, 14*(3), 183–190.

21. Garrison, D. R., Anderson, T., & Archer, W (2001) Critical thinking, cognitive presence, and computer conferencing in distance education. *American Journal of Distance Education, 15*(1), 7–23. https://doi.org/10.1080/08923640109527071

22. Ritter, M., & Lemke, K. (2000). Addressing "the seven principles for good practice in undergraduate education" with internet-enhanced education. *Journal of Geography in Higher Education, 24*(1), 100–108. http://doi.org/10.1080/03098260085171

23. Orcutt, J. M., & Dringus, L. P. (2017). Beyond being there: Practices that establish presence, engage students, and influence intellectual curiosity in structured online learning environment. *Online Learning, 21*(3), 15–35.

24. Jackson, S. H. (2019). Student questions: A path to engagement and social presence in the online classroom. *Journal of Educators Online, 16*(1), 1–8.

25. Kozan, K., & Richardson, J. C. (2014). Interrelationships between and among social, teaching and cognitive presence. *The Internet and Higher Education, 21*, 68–73.

26. Gunawardena, C. N., Lowe, C., & Anderson, T. (1997). Interaction analysis of a global online debate and the development of a constructivist interaction analysis model for computer conferencing. *Journal of Educational Computing Research, 17*, 395–429.

27. Cornell, D., Shukla, K., & Konold, T. R. (2016). Authoritative school climate and student academic engagement, grades, and aspirations in middle and high Schools. *AERA Open, 2*(2), 1–18.

28. Dewey, J. (1938). *Education and experience*. Collier Books.

29. Whiteside, A. L. (2015). Introducing the social presence model to explore online and blended learning experiences. *Online Learning, 19*(2), 53–72.

30. Whiteside, A. L. (2015). Introducing the social presence model to explore online and blended learning experiences. *Online Learning, 19*(2), 53–72.

31. Dikkers, A. G., Whiteside, A. L., & Lewis, S. (2013). Virtual high school teacher and student reactions to the social presence model. *Journal of Interactive Online Learning, 12*(3), 156–170.

32. Eteokleous, N., Ktoridou, D., & Orphanou, M. (2014). Integrating wikis as educational tools for the development of a community of inquiry. *American Journal of Distance Education, 28*(2), 103–116.

33. Dikkers, A. G., Whiteside, A. L., & Lewis, S. (2013). Virtual high school teacher and student reactions to the social presence model. *Journal of Interactive Online Learning, 12*(3), 156–170.

34. Cox-Davenport, R. A. (2014). A grounded theory of faculty's use of humanization to create online course climate. *Journal of Holistic Nursing, 32*(1), 16–24.

35. Jackson, L. C., Jones, S. J., & Rodriguez, R. C. (2010). Faculty actions that result in student satisfaction in online courses. *Journal of Asynchronous Learning Networks, 14*(4), 78–96.

36. Ke, F. (2010). Examining online teaching, cognitive, and social presence for adult students. *Computers & Education, 55*, 808–820.

37. Jackson, S. H. (2019). Student questions: A path to engagement and social presence in the online classroom. *Journal of Educators Online, 16*(1), 1–8.

38. Jackson, S. H. (2019). Student questions: A path to engagement and social presence in the online classroom. *Journal of Educators Online, 16*(1), 1–8.

39. Dewey, J. (1938). *Education and experience.* Collier Books.

40. Chickering, A. W., & Gamson, Z. F. (1987). Seven principles for good practice in undergraduate education. *The Wingspread Journal, 9*(2), 3–7.

41. Whiteside, A. L. (2015). Introducing the social presence model to explore online and blended learning experiences. *Online Learning, 19*(2), 53–72.

42. Nishikant, S. (2009). The paradigm shift for adult education: From educational slavery to learning freedom of human brain with synaptic learning. In T. Kidd (Ed.), *Online* education and adult learning: New frontiers for teaching practices (pp. 150–164). IGI Global.

43. Garrison, D. R., Anderson, T., & Archer, W. (2001). Critical thinking, cognitive presence, and computer conferencing in distance education. *American Journal of Distance Education, 15*(1), 7–23. https://doi.org/10.1080/08923640109527071

44. Faust, P. B., Ennis, L. S., & Hodge, W. M. (2014). The relationship between middle grade student belonging and middle grade student performance. *Alabama Journal of Educational Leadership, 1*, 43–54.

Chapter 5

Student Sense of Belonging

Student sense of belonging is a critical segment of the meaningful and productive teacher-student relationship. Teachers must foster a sense of belonging in each learner, as the classroom, whether virtual or brick-and-mortar, is the home away from home of many students. Being cognizant of a sense of belonging makes a student feel comfortable and allows for a setting in which that student can effectively engage with the class and with the curriculum.

The nurturing of student sense of belonging has been found to lead to positive academic and social consequences. It is common that a student is unable to succeed in secondary and postsecondary school if they do not develop a strong sense of belonging.[1] Historically, student sense of belonging has been recognized as a vital component to student success. From as early as 1962, Maslow shared that the development of a sense of belonging was more important to human development than was the requirement for knowledge and understanding.[2]

Acceptance is essential in the development of meaningful student sense of belonging. Sense of belonging should include feelings of being accepted, valued, included, and encouraged by others in the classroom.[3] The feeling of being recognized as an important member of the community is central to sense of belonging.

Sense of belonging is not simply student realization of friendships, as it encompasses encouragement and esteem for a student's personal autonomy, for the student's ideas, and for the student as an individual. In deconstructing this idea, research has shown that sense of belonging comprises two key attributes. First, it involves feelings of being accepted, needed, and valued. Second, it includes feelings of fitting in and being connected to a group, class, subject, institution, or all of these.[4] Fostering this connectedness is a challenge that the teacher in a virtual environment must identify and address.

Student sense of belonging has been found to be a factor in academic achievement. Great importance should be placed on the sense of belonging a student feels in a classroom, as that sense of belonging is directly linked to academic success. Sense of belonging is more than simply observing the reality that one is liked or feels personal warmth from others. Rather, it also involves a perceived respect for and confirmation of personal autonomy, ultimately regarding the student as an individual and as a valued member of the class. This need for belonging has been found to be a necessity for all students if they are expected to function satisfactorily in any type of learning environment.[5]

For many students, the importance of having an established sense of belonging, with regard to their schools, coursework, teachers, and peer groups has been found to be critically vital to academic success and in inspiring student perseverance.[6] The link between student sense of belonging and enhanced student academic and social engagement and academic success has been found to increase student self-worth.[7] Effective teacher-student relationships foster the creation of a strong sense of belonging, allowing the student to realize confidence, respect, and ultimately, academic success.

As discussed previously, in virtual environments, teachers are rarely, if ever, physically present in the lives of students. One of the main disadvantages of virtual learning is the lack of physical presence and in-person interaction. This problem is amplified when working with students of special learning styles such as those who are tactile or kinesthetic learners, using movement, touch, and activity in learning. Lack of teacher-student interaction is a barrier and an obstacle to learning.[8] The ways in which teachers plan for the absence of physical presence during teacher-student interaction in a virtual setting is an important determining factor when considering student motivation and overall academic success. Student self-confidence, self-efficacy, and self-esteem become augmented when teachers make the effort to create meaningful and productive teacher-student relationships.

Research has found that it is during adolescence that teacher-student relationships become crucial in terms of establishing and fostering student sense of belonging.[9] Supporting this idea, we have discovered that the direction and aid facilitated by educational stakeholders is crucial during adolescence, as many students do not receive support of this nature elsewhere.[10] This type of support affords some students the opportunity to improve their educational trajectories.

THE ROLE OF COMMUNITIES OF INQUIRY ON STUDENT SENSE OF BELONGING

Student sense of belonging is somewhat dependent on the actions of all educational stakeholders who contribute to the community of inquiry. Fitting in, being accepted, and connected in the classroom, as well as feeling respect from teachers and peers, all ultimately contribute to the bolstering of student sense of belonging. Each of these slices of sense of belonging can prove to be more challenging in a virtual setting than in a brick-and-mortar environment, as observed with Moore's transactional distance theory.[11]

It is a challenge for teachers in virtual environments to nurture a student sense of belonging, as the teacher and student rarely, if ever, see one another in-person. I can't stress the importance of that dynamic enough. Thus, the community becomes essential to sense of belonging. Virtual education has been described as a cooperative experience that embraces a sense of belonging and acceptance in a group with common interests.[12] Further, it has been observed that throughout history, there has been a general necessity to belong. The need to work together has always been fundamental to human achievement.[13] The community of inquiry is crucial to learning in both the virtual environment and the brick-and-mortar classroom, as every educational stakeholder has a role in the community. However, due to the challenges of the increased transactional distance of the virtual setting, the community of inquiry is needed as a support system for many students who might otherwise become isolated and disengaged.

STUDENT SENSE OF BELONGING AS A TEACHING AND LEARNING TOOL

Much like teacher presence and student engagement, to be effective, student sense of belonging is best nurtured when built into the lesson planning, especially in a virtual environment, where increased transactional distance can be a significant challenge. Valuable approaches for creating and nurturing a sense of belonging in any school environment should embrace activities that have been purposefully designed to foster connectedness, while facilitating collaboration amongst the entire school community.[14] This plan for a whole school approach is necessary for the construction of student sense of belonging.[15]

Every student's sense of belonging should be promoted through deliberate lesson designs that are mindful of school climate and culture. Student sense of belonging is enriched when teachers recognize and nurture adaptive academic and relational viewpoints in the learning environment.[16] In looking at the whole school approach, the school environment is at its best when supportive, with safe spaces that allow students the opportunity to consult with and get assistance from a trusted and nonjudgmental adult. There can be a potential problem with this notion, however, as this plan has exposed a point of conflict, as the occasional teacher is unwilling or incapable of working outside of normal teaching routines or is unwilling to offer supplemental student assistance, or real, meaningful, face-to-face time.[17]

The reality is, however, that the job of a middle school teacher who teaches virtually is already above and beyond the norm, in terms of answering the call of establishing creative student opportunities for success. It's just plain hard to be successful in this model without going above and beyond. The facilitation of opportunities and a climate conducive to the nurturing of student sense of belonging create a big piece of this puzzle. Teachers who are mindful of student sense of belonging understand that a planned and deliberate emphasis on belonging could be the difference between student success and student failure.

You might be thinking that the ideas in this section would have worked in support of the social presence segment, as well. . . . and you would be correct. Again, many of the concepts that emerged through this study were found to cross over amongst the big ideas.

As mentioned, strong student sense of belonging is linked to positive academic outcomes. Thus, it makes sense that inadequate student sense of belonging would be connected to decreased student academic success. When the necessary sense of belonging is not attained, substantial negative outcomes usually follow, including an academic effect. Consequently, a student's academic potential may not be realized when they do not feel as though to be part of the team.

For students whose self-identities are vulnerable, any amplification of challenging dynamics can make them susceptible to disengagement. The increased transactional distance of the virtual classroom setting is one such factor. The potential for disengagement in the virtual setting means that a student's sense of belonging at school is more likely to be compromised, causing that student to drift, academically.

The nurturing of a strong student sense of belonging has been found to be helpful in the retaining of students who are, otherwise, vulnerable to leaving school. There should be no higher aspirational goal of an educational stakeholder than the fostering of student success. Comprehensive student success is an elusive goal that might never be fully realized. However, when student sense of belonging is a respected and deliberate piece of daily instruction, educators are better able to position each student one step closer to success.

STUDENT SENSE OF BELONGING'S ROLE IN THE ACADEMICS OF THE WHOLE CHILD

Like teacher presence and student engagement, student sense of belonging holds a significant stake in student academic success. A positive correlation has been found regarding student sense of belonging in school, as well as outside of the classroom, in helping to foster student success.[18] In this regard, the social aspect of school interaction is as or more important than the academic.

The classroom would seem the perfect environment in which to put forth the effort to improve student academic success through any available means. Still, while research has found that student sense of belonging is an indispensable human need that reliably connects to self-esteem, acceptance, academic success, and constructive interpersonal relationships in middle school years, teaching plans focusing on sense of belonging are rarely found in the classroom.[19] Hence, the addition of an emphasis on student sense of belonging into the curriculum could reap not only academic rewards but also social-emotional rewards, ultimately allowing students the opportunity to realize greater learning potential.

Attention paid to the whole child, beyond academics, is crucial to student learning. In observing the whole child, the idea emerges that middle school is known to be a time of real vulnerability in which students challenge values, norms, and self-esteem. Further, middle school is a time in which students tend to seek out approval from other educational stakeholders. Students who do not develop a healthy sense of belonging are regularly susceptible to risky behavior, such as joining gangs, dropping out of school, or abusing drugs.[20] A broad range of physical maturity and fluctuating rates of development create additional challenges for many adolescents.[21]

These challenges can affect student sense of belonging and, ultimately, student success. A lack in student sense of belonging in middle school students has been linked to an increased likelihood for risky behaviors. Thus, student sense of belonging is important to student academic success and to the overall social-emotional well-being of each child. Researchers Deci and Ryan[22] shared that a sense of belonging could potentially:

> meaningfully stimulate students' attentiveness in school, and increase classroom engagement, self-concept, the idea of intrinsic value, and the pursuit of positive academic and social goals and behaviors.

Hearkening back to the concepts of teacher presence and student engagement, it is now understood that to support student sense of belonging, students and teachers must communicate ideas with one another, while respectfully sharing ideas and valuing student input in a way the student is able to observe.

Students' collaborative relationships, sense of self and voice, and school satisfaction may be furthered through positive communication and through the support and embracing of student individualities. Teachers need to focus attention in class on deliberate development of the student identity, student self-esteem, and student sense of belonging. The educational community found in the middle school classroom that tends to appreciate, address, and challenge the whole child, as well as the student, often finds greater academic success.

The incorporation of student views and voices into classroom policies and practices may improve learning experiences. The need for meaningful and productive teacher-student relationships needs to be reinforced and addressed through the implementation of student sense of belonging practices. Ultimately, for student sense of belonging to improve, teacher-student relationships must be meaningful and lasting. The teacher is vital to the construction of student sense of belonging.

A healthy student sense of belonging often leads to improved self-esteem and, ultimately, improved academic success in school. Student sense of belonging is more than a student simply fitting in with peers, as feeling accepted and connected by all educational stakeholders, as well as the teacher's planning in the classroom, can lead to a better overall school experience. Moore's transactional distance theory teaches that increased transactional distance, as found in the virtual classroom environment, can make it difficult to foster a student sense of belonging.[23] Thus, to the teacher establishing student sense of belonging in a virtual setting can be a challenging task.

To help bolster sense of belonging in the virtual classroom, an active community of inquiry is a necessary piece of the equation. Effective online learning should be a collaborative experience, which must include a student sense of belonging and acceptance in a group that shares common interests. Due to the challenges of the increased transactional distance of the virtual setting, the community of inquiry is needed as a support system for many students who might otherwise become disengaged.

To realize a meaningful and lasting effect academically, and for the social-emotional well-being of the whole child, student sense of belonging must be deliberately built into a teacher's lesson planning, especially in a virtual environment. To create a sense of belonging, teachers must design activities that explicitly build teacher-student and student-student connections, while fostering interactions among educational stakeholders across the educational community.

Student sense of belonging is emboldened when the teacher plans for academic and personal interactions tailored to a specific classroom environment.[24] The academic environment needs to be supportive, facilitating nonjudgmental conversations with adults in safe spaces. A positive correlation has been found between students' sense of belonging in school and positive outcomes in and out of the classroom. Again, the research has shown that the social aspect of teacher-student interactions outweighs teacher academic presence in terms of student satisfaction and success. Deliberate actions meant to strengthen student sense of belonging also produce the desired effect of building strong teacher-student relationships.

Academic student success is fundamentally interwoven with student sense of belonging, as decreased sense of belonging shows a strong connection to lowered student academic success.[25] Research has shown that students with marginalized identities have displayed a heightened likelihood of disengaging in school while engaging in risky behavior. It is crucial that educators nurture a strong student sense of belonging, as students who are cognizant of teacher and peer appreciation of their contributions and identify as accepted and respected members of the learning community have shown a lowered risk of dropping out of school.[26] Student sense of belonging knows a strong correlation with positive academic results. When teachers treat sense of belonging as a deliberate piece of daily instruction, the students are better able move one step closer to academic success.

Sense of belonging is essential not only to student academic success but also to the overall social-emotional well-being of each child. Classroom engagement, self-esteem, positive social behaviors, and the concept of the intrinsic value of education are often reinforced when teacher planning deliberately focuses on student sense of belonging. Teachers need to focus attention in class on nurturing the students' identities, self-worth, and sense of belonging.

When student voices are included in teacher planning, as well as in classroom policies, and when teachers deliberately address the whole child, as well as the academic developmental needs of students, student academic success often follows. Obviously, student success is at the forefront of positive schooling efforts. Development of student sense of belonging at this crucial stage could potentially keep a child from dropping out of school or causing self-harm through risky behaviors.

If academic success comes two years later, so be it. Delaying academic success is not the end of the world. In this case, at least the child is still in school. We talk a lot about academic success, which is greatly important, but we often seem to want it now, with no delay. Our attitude is often one of: *If I teach this, the student will learn it.* Instant gratification serves our egos well. However, sometimes just helping to facilitate student sense of belonging can bridge a gap between this year and next, allowing for greater future success.

The need for meaningful and long-lasting teacher-student relationships has been reinforced through the analysis of student sense of belonging. Building meaningful and productive student relationships in the virtual classroom may be challenging but is ultimately necessary to student success and health of the whole child. The fostering of a healthy sense of belonging when central to the planning of every teacher in a virtual setting could be the most important component in the development and ultimate success of each child.

As teacher presence and student engagement develop, student sense of belonging takes shape, contributing to student academic success and to the forming of the teacher-student relationship. Student sense of belonging is not only the idea of simply fitting in with peers, rather it hinges on a student finding an identity in the school community. Feeling accepted and connected in the classroom can, and often does, lead to a better overall experience at school. For a teacher, working to establish student sense of belonging in a virtual setting can be a challenging task. As Moore's transactional distance theory states, increased transactional distance, such as that of the virtual classroom environment, can make the fostering of student sense of belonging a challenge.[27]

To help bolster sense of belonging in the virtual classroom, the active community of inquiry is a necessary piece of the equation, as students tend to perform better when they are allowed the opportunity to become involved in the educational community.

Like teacher presence and student engagement, student sense of belonging must be built into the lesson planning of the teacher, especially in a virtual environment. Effectual approaches to fostering student sense of belonging in the virtual classroom include planning for learning that is explicitly designed to build connectedness and helping to cultivate interaction among the whole school community. Student sense of belonging is improved when each teacher promotes academic and interpersonal contexts tailored to a specific classroom environment. Thus, teacher presence, student engagement, and student sense of belonging each contribute to student academic success and to the formation of meaningful and productive teacher-student relationships.

Academic success as well as the health of the whole child are fundamentally interwoven with student sense of belonging. Much like teacher presence and student engagement, decreased sense of belonging shows a strong connection to lowered student academic success. However, student sense of belonging is tied not only to academics but also to the self-worth of the whole child. Middle schoolers necessitate encouragement and respect from fellow students, as well as from teachers and other adult educational stakeholders, as these positive interactions are crucial to social-emotional development. Teachers need to focus attention in class on student identity and self-esteem development, as well as fostering of student sense of belonging, as those elements of each student influence the whole child.

When teacher presence, student engagement, and student sense of belonging are brought together, the positive result is often one of student academic success and the nurturing of the whole child and effective and caring teacher-student relationships. The literature points directly to the need for teachers in a virtual setting to unambiguously plan for presence, for active and meaningful student engagement, and for the fostering of student sense of belonging. When planning explicitly addresses these areas of teaching, and when the teacher follows through on the planning, student academic success and the nurturing of teacher-student relationships is more easily facilitated.

By tapping into the stories of middle school teachers who teach virtually, I was able to collect much needed information regarding the ways in which each teacher utilizes teacher presence, nurtures student engagement, and fosters a sense of belonging in the student who learns virtually to build meaningful and productive teacher-student relationships in the virtual classroom.

FOSTERING STUDENT SENSE OF BELONGING IN THE VIRTUAL MIDDLE SCHOOL ENVIRONMENT

Student sense of belonging is essential in all classroom environments but is especially so in virtual environments. As the virtual classroom environment can be one of isolation and loneliness, middle school teachers in the virtual classroom need to create opportunities for the development of comradery among students. As shared by the participants in this study, when a student feels that they are a part of a team, they will usually perform better academically. This finding is supported by the research that has explicitly linked student sense of belonging to academic success and found student sense of belonging to be a necessity for all students if they are expected to function productively in school.

Belonging and knowing that oneself is acknowledged as a team member increases morale, engagement, and the likelihood of academic success. Thus, it falls to the virtual teacher to create opportunities for student involvement, both socially and academically. Opportunities for the development of student sense of belonging also help in the construction of meaningful and productive teacher-student relationships in the virtual middle-school environment.

STUDENT SENSE OF BELONGING IN THE VIRTUAL CLASSROOM: TEACHER RESPONSES

Hand in hand with student safety is the concept of student sense of belonging. As the participants in this study discussed the creation of safe spaces in the virtual classroom in which students are given the opportunity to succeed, these middle school teachers also told their stories of fostering student sense of belonging.

Here, the educators shared not only their thoughts on student sense of belonging but also their techniques for ensuring that each student is given the opportunity to play an active role in the community. Ultimately, to succeed, students need to feel welcome and accepted, and each must comprehend the idea that every student is an important part of the community, including oneself.

Recently, VIVA has begun to implement the use of cameras into everyday teaching. While the software being used, Newrow, has not been without its problems, overall, the students genuinely enjoy seeing each other. The use of cameras has been a boost for the construction of the classroom community, thus bolstering student opportunities for active participation in each virtual class.

As more students participate and allow themselves to be seen and heard, the greater community grows, allowing for more chances for student sense of belonging. However, when a student is shy or simply does not willingly participate, the teacher must create openings in which student sense of belonging can flourish.

Karen discussed differences in student participation and overall sense of belonging when she stated:

> Some students are comfortable with the virtual environment, and they feel that sense of belonging kind of naturally just by making relationships with their teachers and other students. But others I know don't feel as comfortable with that and probably need socialization outside of the classroom to feel a sense of belonging there.

Karen does not claim to have all the answers, so she reaches out to the students to try to facilitate their sense of belonging. She shared:

> I have brought this up to students in the past, like: "what could I do to make you feel more comfortable in this class to talk with each other?" But it's always a certain group of students that I feel more comfortable and feel like they belong in the classroom more than others. And it's been difficult for me to figure out and to pinpoint why it's working for some and why it's not working for others.

Like Karen, Bobbi goes out of her way to make opportunities for students to develop a sense of belonging. Actively recruiting extracurricular participation has been a key reason she has seen the success she has this year as this student involvement centers on sense of belonging.
Bobbi shared:

> I have a very engaged group this year [2020–2021], or whether it's quarantine and they're all just starving for connection, but I feel like this year, they are, they're starving for connection this year. So, I do feel like they feel like part of a group. We've had really good discussions this year in Newrow. Christmas break, a couple of kids were like: "I'll miss you guys so much for the next two

weeks." Just really, I feel like this year has been a really good sense of belonging with maybe a couple of exceptions who I'm still trying to draw into the crowd.

In discussing her facilitation of student sense of belonging, Bobbi stated:

> During conferences, I always say: "What's your talent? What's your gift? What's your hobby?" If they say photography, I'm like: "I really want to see a picture. Text it to me. Email it to me." Then, once you have the picture in your hand, you can say: "Do you mind if I put this up?" And usually, they're like: "No." I've had a couple kids that were like: "Yes, I do mind." Fine. I'm not going to do it against your will. But, I just think getting a student to share something with you opens the door to sharing with more people.

Directly asking students to participate in this manner shows the students that community is important to Bobbi. Student sense of belonging is a by-product of her actions. Thus, the students know she cares about them and about the culture of the class. The active role she takes in facilitating sense of belonging helps in the building of teacher-student relationships.

Much like Bobbi's personal outreach, Jill plants seeds for the development of student sense of belonging. Using examples from her life, she sparks discussion that nurtures student sense of belonging. Jill shared that she feels that sense of belonging has to do with students feeling and understanding that they are on the same team. She stated:

> I'm really trying to encourage reframing that and utilizing the class, the communities, the support practice where they encourage one another. Right? . . . I talked about tacos all the time, so we talk about tacos all the time. We talk about what we like to eat and someone will say: "Oh, I thought about you, Susie, the other day, because you said you like chicken, and I had chicken tacos the other day."

While a discussion on chicken tacos might seem trivial, Jill's technique gets the students thinking outside of the box in an extracurricular way. Students learn about each other and get to know one another as more than just a face on the screen or a voice solving math problems. It is these interactions that Jill relies on to build student sense of belonging. As the students then relate their conversations back to Jill, they understand that she cares about them.

I, too, have utilized tactics such as these. For instance, I once asked students to explain Boba drinks to me. My interest in their expertise led to many students participating, which then carried over into academic participation. Students who had not really established their own sense of belonging turned their cameras on and suddenly became important figures in our discussion. Facilitating these opportunities is imperative in the building of teacher-student relationships.

To foster student sense of belonging, Daisy works with her students outside of the constraints of academia. While her class has been "quiet" this year, Daisy shared ways that she is trying to assist in the creation of student sense of belonging, again placing an emphasis on safety.

> That's again creating a safe environment, letting them or allowing them to chat, but of course monitoring what they're talking about and putting them into . . . I've been trying to do this group thing, small group breakout room thing that has not been very successful and really been trying to foster that environment and we're working hard on that, but just small groups where they interact more and they feel comfortable. It's just like today for homeroom class connect, we talked about, would you rather go on a Disney cruise, or would you rather go on a tropical paradise trip? I thought: "Oh, this will be something positive that they can talk about." Of course, it was crickets still. I'm just like: "What is happening here? These kids are not talking to each other."

Continuing, Daisy stated:

> There's always a kiddo in class that's going to be messing around, but you just have to make sure that they know it's a safe environment in class and there's no judgment. They're all in there together. I reinforce that topic constantly. We work as a team in here and it's safe in here. We can say what we need to say and there's no judgment. . . . so that's kind of the environment that I'm trying to foster is for them to get to know each other and to feel safe.

Daisy has created opportunities for students to communicate before and during class, in hopes that social engagement will lead to academic engagement, also helping to establish student sense of belonging. While engagement has been a recent challenge for Daisy, she continues to use team-building techniques, sometimes resorting to what she considers to be bribery.

> The kids all log in fifteen minutes early every time and I let them chat. I always monitor their chat, but I let them chat to get to know each other and that's huge. Once they start to get to know each other, they start to feel more comfortable, they start to feel more comfortable grabbing the mic. I still haven't yet started the point system, but it's almost like you have to, I don't like to say it's bribery, but sometimes it seems like you kind of have to bribe these kids to interact. I did it last year with Starbucks cards. I haven't started it yet, but I'm going to do extra credit, I think, for kids that grab the mic and participate.

In keeping her virtual classroom a safe environment, Daisy is quick to address inappropriate behavior.

Just reiterating the fact that it's a safe environment. They can give me a sad face if it doesn't make sense. There's no judgment in class, period. There's none and they know that if someone does that, then I won't point out anybody's name or do anything, but if I see something negative come through chat, I'll say: "That is not appropriate." . . . I'll just say: "We need to stay on topic," because the other kids get frustrated too sometimes when someone's off topic.

Ultimately, Daisy has been frustrated by the overall silence of her class this year and with the vexations this silence has presented to her hopes of an engaged class. Still, through her planned safety measures and the lure of peer friendship, and even the occasional gift card, Daisy keeps working toward the nurturing of increased participation, as she realizes the importance of granting the opportunity for all students to feel a sense of belonging. These measures also help Daisy in the building of strong and meaningful teacher-student relationships.

Joy also finds student sense of belonging to be of great importance. She shared that student sense of belonging is often more important than is academic success in that students need a community, and each member of that community is essential. Joy stated:

If you're in Mrs. C's class, it's important. You're important in here, and we need you. We can't do this without any of you. So, making sure that they feel a sense of belonging gives them an investment into the success of that group. If you were on a team, you would want to make sure that you're doing your part to pull it forward. And so my first rule in my classroom is always respect each other. That's the most important thing, even above turning in your work and all that kind of stuff.

Like Daisy, Joy has little patience for inappropriate or counterproductive communication in her virtual classroom, so she works to counter the negativity that is otherwise ubiquitous in online interaction. Joy shared:

[What is important is] respecting each other and making sure that we all feel like we are a community. You cannot disrespect that person without getting called out, or you can't tell somebody: "that's stupid." No. That's disrespectful. You may not agree with it, but we're not going to tolerate any of that. So, I think at first it seemed really foreign to them because the internet is full of communities that are really awful, really terrible to each other, and that's how they communicate and they get stuck in that loop of I make fun of you and that's how I relate to you. So, we try and really make sure that they understand in our environment. We're just respectful, encouraging, supportive of each other. That doesn't mean we never disagree, but it means that we're going to do it in a respectful way.

Joy sees her middle school virtual classroom as a safe, positive space, valuing community, safety, and sense of belonging, even above academic results. For her, the classroom is a place her students can go to interact in a positive and productive manner. Her students know that the classroom community is important to her. She stresses the importance of student participation and community each day. In this way, Joy has built, and continues to build strong and meaningful teacher-student relationships.

In discussing student sense of belonging in the virtual classroom, Mike shared the difficulties of gauging whether a student really feels as though they are a part of the class community. Continuing, Mike also acknowledged that students all come from "a different background" and that some students simply prefer to be spectators rather than participants in class. Mike shared:

> I think it depends on the students themselves. Some of them are used to interacting with other students and feeling like they're a part of a classroom. Some just like to sit there and watch. At the same time, they probably feel as if they're a part of a classroom as well. It's just difficult to gauge all the time.

Mike somewhat equated the happiness of students in seeing one another to being the closest measurement he has found in gauging student sense of belonging. He stated:

> You accept that as them engaging in the classroom and engaging with their fellow students, and things like that. The happier they are, they're happy to see each other or engage with each other, there's an actual visual thing that you can see, that they're enjoying the environment and they're happy.

Mike shared some of the challenges in establishing student sense of belonging when he discussed lack of student engagement.

> Some of the challenges are . . . Sometimes the student doesn't engage, and that's really challenging, or the engagement is limited. I have a lot of students who do not like to use a mic or video, and so their level of participation is low. It might just be through a chat service. Even though they're engaged, it's not at the level that I hoped that it could be. Sometimes they're just engaged with each other in order to communicate with each other. That gets a little bit challenging too, because now you're redirecting, or at least trying to redirect. You want them to be there, and at the same time you want them to be happy and to enjoy it, but you also want them focused. That can be challenging.

Ultimately, like the other teachers in this study, Mike has neither an answer that is 100% sure to engage all students nor has he been able to create a guaranteed system for fostering student sense of belonging in the virtual classroom. However, his best practices have resulted in encouraging results.

No two classrooms are alike, and Mike has worked to provide opportunities for his students to establish friendships, community, and a sense of belonging. While he strives for a better way to gauge student sense of belonging, he continues to build meaningful and productive teacher-student relationships.

Like the other participants of the study, Tammy shared that she believes that student sense of belong is: "highly, highly important" stating that the students: "need to feel like they're part of a class and part of a community." Where she differed from her colleagues in this study is her strict philosophy of keeping work separate from her private life. Tammy shared:

> I talk about my class being like our classroom family. Some of the members are a little strange. Some of them you don't really want to talk to you outside of class. But when we're here, we're a family. We're all together. We're sharing everything that we all know, sharing knowledge, sharing learning, and that's how I foster it.

When asked to discuss the ways in which she has approached her own fostering of student sense of belonging, Tammy shared that she has encouraged her: "students to join clubs," stating: "We have a lot of extracurricular clubs." Tammy's approach is neither as direct nor as personal as the other teachers. However, she did discuss the concept of the class environment as a family. This identification of the classroom family is key to the building of meaningful and productive teacher-student relationships.

All the participants in this study deemed student sense of belonging as being greatly important in terms of supporting the student as a whole child, as well as in the academic success of students. Describing their classes as families and teams, the participants told stories of activities they have implemented that have fostered student sense of belonging, as well as some activities that did not work as well as hoped.

In working to nurture sense of belonging, the participants mentioned utilizing cameras, microphones, chat, private chat, special homeroom activities, birthday activities, point systems, and outright bribery. The increased student engagement that is spawned from these activities is the direct result of opportunities that have been deliberately generated by each teacher. When students feel they are a part of a team or a family, they tend to engage more and pay closer attention to what is happening in class. Also, when the students see the teacher working hard to facilitate such team-building activities, the process itself goes a long way in establishing meaningful and productive teacher-student relationships in the virtual middle school classroom.

Student sense of belonging was discussed as having great importance on both the whole child and on the academic productivity of each student. When students feel that they belong in class and are comfortable and safe in the classroom setting, they are free to succeed. The use of cameras, microphones, games, and social time were each mentioned by the participants of this study as being crucial in nurturing student sense of belonging. The use of cameras was described by six of the participants in this study as integral to building productive and meaningful teacher-student relationships in virtual settings.

VIRTUAL TEACHERS' FOSTERING OF STUDENT SENSE OF BELONGING IN THE VIRTUAL ENVIRONMENT

The storytelling of the participants in this study supported the findings of the literature on student sense of belonging. Central to the stories of the participants in this study was the sense of urgency regarding student sense of belonging in building meaningful and productive teacher-student relationships, especially when teaching in the virtual environment.

The teachers in this study shared the ways in which they grant opportunities for the emergence of student sense of belonging. From hosting virtual talent shows to sharing conversational prompts on nonacademic topics, to giving participation points for virtual nonacademic chats, to bluntly telling the students that they are important members of a team, the teachers in this study discussed the cruciality of facilitating opportunities for the establishment of student sense of belonging.

Supporting the data from the teachers in this study, the research showed that student sense of belonging also tended to comprise respect for individuals while granting opportunities for autonomy and deference for the whole child. The participants in this study found that when feelings of respect from the teacher's efforts to create a real team in which every student is appreciated and, further, when that respect is recognized as sincere by the student, then the building blocks of academic success were sure to be established.

The literature and findings in this study support one another in regarding student sense of belonging as a crucial element in student success, as well as in the building of meaningful and productive teacher-student relationships in the virtual environment. Looking back to 1962, Maslow[28] found sense of belonging to be more important to human development than the requirement for knowledge and understanding. Similarly, we have discovered that human achievement has historically centered on belonging and collaboration.

Academically speaking, when the needed sense of belonging is not achieved, there may be substantial deleterious outcomes, including a negative academic impact. This lack of sense of belonging is one of the instances in which we see students disengage from their own educational opportunities, thus putting them at risk for dropping out of school and engaging in risky behaviors. On the positive side of this idea, an important correlation has been unearthed. This correlation links student sense of belonging to favorable results in not only school but also in the life after school. The research and the literature each point to student sense of belonging as crucial to success.

MORE ON STUDENT SAFETY

The concept of student safety emerged in the stories of nearly every participant. Student safety in the virtual environment refers to the facilitation of an established comfort with the teacher such that it encourages the student to participate or at least engage on some level with the teacher, as well as with the content, without fear of unnecessary backlash or mockery.

Teachers in this study shared stories of private messaging shy students or calling them after class to ask if they would be willing to participate in class the next day. This communication would be completed before the teacher called on them in class so as not to put the student on the spot. The reason for calling the student was not simply to avoid embarrassing them but also to establish the idea of a safe learning space in which a student could thrive without fear of ridicule.

Supporting this idea, the research suggested that the school environment is at its best when supportive, replete with safe spaces that allow students the opportunity to consult with a trusted adult, and where they can receive assistance without being harshly judged.[29] This notion was reiterated by the participants in this study as the idea of interacting in a positive manner with students while never embarrassing them was central to student safety, sense of belonging and, ultimately, the building of meaningful and productive teacher-student relationships in virtual environments.

One critical element of virtual learning is student-student communication, as these interactions significantly influence both social and academic exchanges with the teacher, the curriculum and the course itself.[30] Educational and social teacher-student, student-student, and student-content exchanges are critical considerations in the comprehensive delivery of information, as well as in the enhancement of teaching quality and in the communication of directions. Interaction in online education has a direct impact on the level of student satisfaction.[31] Thus, when students are disconnected from classmates and teachers, this satisfaction may decrease. This is where student sense of belonging comes into play. When a student is able to identify as an important part of the learning team, they will perform better, academically.

It is up to the virtual teacher to create opportunities for fostering student sense of belonging. Teacher-student interaction is important in nurturing student interest in course content. This interaction has also been found to stimulate student academic motivation. Thus, interaction is an important facet in overall student academic achievement.

The virtual setting itself has been found to be a hindrance to some students. Students have reported feelings of loneliness and anxiety, as they find the virtual classroom to be an alien learning space.[32] Students have also described feelings of insecurity in terms of their ability to succeed in the isolation that is known to be a part of the virtual environment experience. Further, many students view the notion of virtual interaction with other virtual students to be intimidating and regard virtual teamwork as threatening. These feelings of inadequacy have the potential to hinder a student's sense of belonging, which then impacts their ability to succeed academically.

While teacher presence, student sense of belonging, and student engagement are each key pieces of the construction of teacher-student relationships, other common elements of student readiness must be considered when studying the overall effectiveness of virtual classrooms.

In discussing the significance of classroom interaction, our participants deliberated on various factors that may affect student success in a virtual environment. Some of those factors include student self-efficacy, fluctuating levels of readiness and computer literacy, behavior when interacting, age and ethnicity, learning style, cultural diversity, and student attitude to distance and online learning. A teacher has a lot to consider when planning for social and academic presence and interaction. No pressure!

FROM THE PD!

During my recent professional development, I asked my fellow teachers how they go about nurturing a student sense of belonging. The responses are below. Again, names have been removed.

How Do You Nurture Student Sense of Belonging in Your Live Sessions?

> Tell them how important they are to our class . . . on a daily basis
> We are real . . . good days and bad days and we are in this thing together
> I love saying their name when they enter.
> Kids help each other and are very supportive of each other. They all listen and show interest in each other's thoughts
> not for nothing-I laugh at their jokes. I think it helps!

"We still need ___ to participate" as if it's a team effort, we are all in this together!
share vulnerable insights during discussions
Fostering a community for peers to help peers
I select students to read randomly with my deck of cards—then take as long as it takes to draw them out and convince them to talk.
Encourage students to greet each other and connect with each other as well
Share their passions outside of school
Celebrating wins
PJ party
I share with them how difficult MS was because I didn't speak English (ELS)
They love those personal teacher stories
We have birthday celebrations

When Turning on Cameras, What Happens?

Most of them are terribly shy
Or a student turns on their mic and there is TONS of background noise
they are embarrassed
I understand why they can't focus!!
There is a younger sibling on the lap of my student.
I was just going to say that. No wonder they can't focus. I don't get why the parents don't respect that
Some are still in bed in HRCC. I say that's okay I am just so happy you are here.
It's give and take. SOME students are more open online because they're hiding behind a screen. Some kids who never would share in person, shy/anxiety, do online
it is why I really miss CD
Students introduce their siblings
one on one breakout rooms when I notice a student is having a bad day
Just chat on camera. It lowers their anxiety.
Pet days, texts to families and students, checking in often
I allow siblings to play blooket with us or as a team with the student
Yes, we will pause everything to say hi to a sibling or pet.
Students with younger siblings on their laps.
I see lots of ceiling fans lol
Yup more than the amount Home Depot has lol
I make them say Hi and bye to me every day on camera or mic
nice vaulted ceilings!
I see lots of tvs in the background too

I love to notice the pictures on the walls in the background

What Do You Discuss in HRCC?

We have kids answer high interest topics such as which is better Pizza or tacos?
let them know life continues at home. We all have noise and confusion at home.
now kids look for MY cat too
Meet 1:1 with those that don't really interact in the whole class just to check in with them
I compliment them on headbands, hoodies, haircuts, cool backgrounds etc.
praising effort
I make sure that I connect via camera each week with students
set up small groups for students who tend to be shy in large group sessions

Now that we have discussed transactional distance, teacher presence and student sense of belonging, it is time to look at the educational community.

NOTES

1. Peacock, S., & Cowan, J. (2019). Promoting sense of belonging in online learning communities of inquiry in accredited courses. *Online Learning, 23*(2), 67–81.
2. Maslow, A. (1962). *Toward a psychology of being.* Van Nostrand.
3. Goodenow, C. (1993). Classroom belonging among early adolescent students: Relationships to motivation and achievement. *The Journal of Early Adolescence, 13*(1), 21–43.
4. Vaccaro, A., Daly-Cano, M., & Newman, B. M. (2015). A sense of belonging among college students with disabilities: An emergent theoretical model. *Journal of College Student Development, 56*(7), 670–686.
5. Jackson, P., Cashmore, A., & Scott, J. (2010). *Sense of belonging: Background literature.* https://www2.le.ac.uk/offices/ssds/projects/student-retention-project/dissemination/papers-and-publications/Sense%20of%20Belonging%20Lit%20Review.docx
6. Vaccaro, A., Daly-Cano, M., & Newman, B. M. (2015). A sense of belonging among college students with disabilities: An emergent theoretical model. *Journal of College Student Development, 56*(7), 670–686.
7. Thomas, L. (2012). *Building student engagement and belonging at a time of change in higher education.* Paul Hamlyn Foundation.
8. Purarjomandlangrudi, A., Chen, D., & Nguyen, A. (2016). Investigating the drivers of student interaction and engagement in online courses: A study of state-of-the-art. *Informatics in Education, 15*(2), 269–286.

9. Murdock, T. B., Anderman, L. H., & Hodge, S. A. (2000). Middle-grade predictors of students' motivation and behavior in high school. *Journal of Adolescent Research, 15*, 327–351.

10. Dutton Tillery, A., Varjas, K., Meyers, J., & Collins, A. S. (2010). General education teachers' perceptions of behavior management and intervention strategies. *Journal of Positive Behavior Interventions, 12*(2), 86–102. https://doi.org/10.1177/1098300708330879

11. Moore, M. (1993). Theory of transactional distance. In D. Keegan, ed., *Theoretical Principles of Distance Education* (1st ed., pp. 22–38). Routledge.

12. Garrison, D. R., & Arbaugh, J. B. (2007). Researching the community of inquiry framework: Review, issues and future directions. *The Internet and Higher Education, 10*(3), 157–172.

13. Garrison, D. (2017). *E-learning in the 21st century: A community of inquiry framework for research and practice* (3rd ed.). Routledge.

14. Rowe, F., & Stewart, D. (2009). Promoting connectedness through whole school approaches: A qualitative study. *Health Education, 109*, 396–413.

15. Pendergast, D., Allen, J., McGregor, G., & Ronksley-Pavia, M. (2018). Engaging marginalized, "at-risk" middle-level students: a focus on the importance of a sense of belonging at school. *Education Sciences, 8*(3), 1–19.

16. Anderman, L. H. (2003). Academic and social perceptions as predictors of change in middle school students' sense of school belonging. *The Journal of Experimental Education, 72*, 5–22.

17. Rowe, F., & Stewart, D. (2009). Promoting connectedness through whole school approaches: A qualitative study. *Health Education, 109*, 396–413.

18. Doda, N., & Knowles, T. (2008). Listening to the voices of young adolescents. *Middle School Journal, 39*(3), 26–33.

19. Faust, P. B., Ennis, L. S., & Hodge, W. M. (2014). The relationship between middle grade student belonging and middle grade student performance. *Alabama Journal of Educational Leadership, 1*, 43–54.

20. Beck, M., & Malley, J. (2003). Pedagogy of belonging. *The International Child and Youth Care Network.* https://cyc-net.org/cyc-online/cycol-0303-belonging.html

21. Faust, P. B., Ennis, L. S., & Hodge, W. M. (2014). The relationship between middle grade student belonging and middle grade student performance. *Alabama Journal of Educational Leadership, 1*, 43–54.

22. Deci, E. L., & Ryan, R. M. (2008). Facilitating optimal motivation and psychological well-being across life's domains. *Canadian Psychology, 49*(1), 14–23.

23. Moore, M. (1993). Theory of transactional distance. In D. Keegan, ed., *Theoretical Principles of Distance Education* (1st ed., pp. 22–38). Routledge.

24. Pendergast, D., Allen, J., McGregor, G., & Ronksley-Pavia, M. (2018). Engaging marginalized, "at-risk" middle-level students: a focus on the importance of a sense of belonging at school. *Education Sciences, 8*(3), 1–19.

25. Pendergast, D., Allen, J., McGregor, G., & Ronksley-Pavia, M. (2018). Engaging marginalized, "at-risk" middle-level students: a focus on the importance of a sense of belonging at school. *Education Sciences, 8*(3), 1–19.

26. Pendergast, D., Allen, J., McGregor, G., & Ronksley-Pavia, M. (2018). Engaging marginalized, "at-risk" middle-level students: a focus on the importance of a sense of belonging at school. *Education Sciences, 8*(3), 1–19.

27. Moore, M. (1993). Theory of transactional distance. In D. Keegan, ed., *Theoretical Principles of Distance Education* (1st ed., pp. 22–38). Routledge.

28. Maslow, A. (1962). *Toward a psychology of being.* Van Nostrand.

29. Pendergast, D., Allen, J., McGregor, G., & Ronksley-Pavia, M. (2018). Engaging marginalized, "at-risk" middle-level students: a focus on the importance of a sense of belonging at school. *Education Sciences, 8*(3), 1–19.

30. Wanstreet, C. E. (2009). Interaction in online learning environments. *The Perfect Online Course: Best Practices for Designing and Teaching, 7*(4), 399–411.

31. Durrington, V. A., Berryhill, A., & Swafford, J. (2006). Strategies for enhancing student interactivity in an online environment. *College Teaching, 54*(1), 190–193.

32. Baxter, J. (2012). Who am I and what keeps me going? Profiling the distance learning student in higher education. *International Review of Research in Open and Distance Learning, 13*(4), 108–129. https://doi.org/10.19173/irrodl.v13i4.1283

Chapter 6

The Educational Community

The educational stakeholders who ensure the success of each student are essential to the facilitation of that student success. But how do we define the educational community? Who are the people a student relies on for support in the virtual environment? The answer to these questions varies, depending on the person answering. However, the idea that a student needs a functioning educational community is nearly universally agreed on.

Once we get past defining the community, we must turn our attention to the ways in which the members of an educational community work together to support the student, if they do indeed work together. If the members of the educational community are not working well together, how does the teacher facilitate stronger support? These are the issues presented here.

UTILIZING THE EDUCATIONAL COMMUNITY IN THE VIRTUAL ENVIRONMENT

While the educational community varies from student to student and classroom environment to classroom environment, the community is often defined as the group of educational stakeholders who directly support a given student. The people identified as the educational community for a given student in the virtual classroom setting play a crucial role in ensuring student engagement and, ultimately, the success of the student.

While the perceived size and scope of the educational community differs from teacher to teacher, each of the participants in this study passionately proclaimed the importance of the middle school student's support team, while sharing stories of the triumphs of students with strong supports at school and at home and the challenges of students who were found to be too isolated at home for success in the virtual classroom environment. Along these lines, the literature supported the participants' findings of the importance of the educational community in the success of the student, citing the fact that students who were isolated and disengaged in middle school were vulnerable to leaving high school before graduating and had started to make the decision to drop out of school in middle-school.[1] Likewise, students who were isolated and disengaged were more likely to abuse drugs and engage in risky behaviors.[2]

Teachers who help a student define their support team and then communicate regularly with that support team often produce students who are engaged and productive, whereas students who cannot identify a reliable educational community often struggle with isolation and disengagement. The act of helping virtual students identify and nurture the educational community also assists in the building of meaningful and productive teacher-student relationships in virtual environments.

Members of the Educational Community

Each participant was asked to discuss the educational community. Identifying the members of the community was the first task. Members of the educational community, or community of inquiry, are those individuals who assist in the facilitation of student learning, whether directly or indirectly. Jill identified the members as such:

> So, first and foremost, it's the students. I think it's the families, whatever that looks like for the kid, as we know that's different. I think that our administration is a part of that, and I think our community is.

Jill went on to discuss the necessary respect for the value of education that is sometimes missing in society.

> I think that one of the things that I've noticed in our society today is that the people really struggle with this value of learning, right? . . . that community belief that education matters for all, that learning is important in general. I think, makes a huge difference for everybody that it can't just be something that you're dealing with because you're in that . . . we should value it all together.

Joy agreed with Jill on the idea that everyone in the community should be invested in education. She compared each stakeholder's place in the equation to ripples in a pond. When asked about the members of the educational community, Joy stated:

> Everybody is. Every single person is. There's rings, right? It goes out kind of like dropping a stone into the pond. It ripples out. But everybody is involved in the educational community. It starts with the students, the teacher, the learning coach, we're like a little triangle. So, us three are the main group, the teams.

And then there's support teachers, they might have special education teachers . . . or they might have tutors or coaches and things like that . . . I mean the community is invested in the success of these kids because they're going to come up and join the community very soon and be the community. So, society needs to be invested on all levels in education . . . it really takes a team. I mean it takes every one of us. And a lot of times, there's a piece missing, and it was for me when I was growing up and I think that I feel sometimes that I overcompensate for that with my students.

Karen was in full agreement with Jill and Joy, also describing the stakeholders as being positioned in rings of influence, as she expanded her web out to discuss local communities. Karen shared:

I feel like everybody should be a part of the educational community. But I think the primary players in the educational community are the teachers, the parents, and the students. Kind of the next ring would be administrators, community members, churches, local businesses. And that actually is different in a virtual space, but in a brick-and-mortar community.

So, I think at the center of the educational community is the families, the teachers, and the students, and then from there it expands a little bit more. I would consider anybody that's in the community, people working at the grocery store. These are all opportunities for education to take place and so I kind of consider them all on different like kind of rings of the education spectrum.

Joy and Karen each observed that education is a public good that should be appreciated by all members of a given community. The feedback given from both teachers is a reminder of their take on the importance of community involvement in education.

Similarly, Bobbi shared that the educational community begins small, as a web in the middle, then expands outward, including not only people but also resources. Then she narrowed the scope tremendously, taking into account a student's immediate support team. Bobbi shared:

I think all the teachers. Obviously, the students. For sure the learning coach and the parent. I have several this year that the learning coach is not a parent. I think other people come into that, too. Siblings and Khan Academy [online education website]. I just think these kids have to draw upon a lot of sources, and a lot of sources have to put energy into the student to make this a really successful environment.

I think at the end of the day, it's the parents no matter what. I think parents followed closely by teacher. I think teachers have a huge impact on the world and on kids, but I think at the end of the day, what you're doing at home and what you're seeing at home and what you're exposed to at home so dramatically affects what you're capable of doing in the classroom.

Bobbi's discussion of each student's home life and the influence it has on the student's actions again recalls one common thread found here in many teachers' wish lists: more personal time with each student.

Members of the Educational Community Working Together or Not

Responsive learning coaches are gold to virtual teachers. Because of this need for communication, many teachers work to establish a relationship with each student's family early on in hopes of nurturing a productive educational community. After identifying the members of the educational community, the participants of this study were asked to discuss the ways in which those community members work together to ensure student success. Answers to this question ranged from examples of absolute cooperation to those of no cooperation. Overall, collaboration was deemed necessary in most cases, as it has been agreed that for most middle school students, a strong support system is crucial to student success.

Jill shared that any student support system would be meaningless unless put into collaborative action. She voiced frustration at what she perceives to be a lack of cooperation among educational stakeholders, as well as a continually lowered valuation of education, in general. In terms of educational stakeholders working together, Jill stated:

> I don't think they are. I think that's our issue. I think that there is some cooperation, but I feel like too many people are focusing on different things. And I think that's why we're having such a breakdown in the learning circle. Right? So, for example, you and I, as educators, are looking at these kids, in this year, at this time, right? You have this many students and those are your children that you're focused on and wanting this individualized growth as you should, right? The teachers are doing that. You're building academic skills.
>
> So, what I keep thinking is that we should have more of that cooperation and keep looking at this as like education is to be valued by all, for everyone in our community, in our society and work together. But we help families who struggle for whatever reason to find resources, to help their students find success through school.
>
> The admin, instead of holding their cards close to their chest, share out with their teachers what's happening because I'm certain that a lot of the things and a lot of policies you're making are in reaction to . . . policies and procedures coming out of state, federal agencies or in anticipation of shifts in student population, shifts in student learning, because we know that, right? . . . and there's very different reasons and different needs. And I think whether it's the neighbor, the grandparent, the neighbor down the street whose kids are all grown and grandkids they're all grown, value education, just as much as me and you who have

small tolerance and everywhere in between, they had all those pieces in places. I think we have a much more cohesive and productive educational system.

I think that families sometimes are looking at education as something they have to put their kids through versus being a part of that process. And there's a myriad of reasons for that. It feels to me so much that there's too much of a veil of secrecy.... and I think if we looked at it more as not community family, not family versus, or student versus teacher, not all these things now, actually, then we're a team and we all play a role like on a basketball team, like on a football team, and that works. I think that's what makes the huge difference.

Jill's statement: "families look at education as something they have to put their kids through" is telling. This response speaks to a segment of society's perception of the education system and shows a critique of the public schools as well as an obvious lack of respect for education. Personally, I have worked with families who have made it clear that school was not a priority. It is a difficult situation that insists on open communication and working with the family to establish specific short- and long-term goals.

Along these lines, Karen agreed with Jill, regarding public sentiment on the topic of education. Furthering the scope of the discussion, she brought public policy into the equation. Both Jill and Karen pointed to public perception of education as problematic, in that when the perception of the system, in general, is one of malignancy, it becomes much easier to criticize or dismiss the efforts of those working in schools. Karen shared:

I think a lot of what's happened politically with education has limited what people see as academic success. So not only do we have disagreement right now on what academic success looks like, but we have disagreement on how to get there and who's responsible and all that kind of stuff. So, I feel like it is important for everybody to work together to promote student academic success, but there's a lot of problems that we have.... if we could at least agree on what academic success is and then just allow that flexibility of how to get there, we might be on the right track. But I feel like there's a lot of streamlining. For whatever reason, policymakers have decided that there's a certain path that everybody has to take to get to this one goal. We can't even agree what that goal is, but we want everybody to take the same path to get there. And that's not really working.

Alright, so I think just in general there has to be an agreement between teacher, student, and parent or guardians, whoever's at home with the student. There has to be agreement between the three that school is important and that's what's going to build the most successful students. When any one of those pieces is missing is when you start to have some issues.

Moving into the virtual space, I think that trio becomes even more important, because in person I think a teacher can take on a little bit more of the load of motivating the student, but once the students are staying at home and they're online, it either has to be all motivation from the student, or the parent is really there helping motivate the student because the teacher doesn't have as much access to kind of push that type of motivation because they're not really . . . obviously we're not in the student's home. We can't force them to turn on a computer. In a classroom we can actually tell them: "No, you need to take out this book. You need to do this now." And you're standing over them.

Karen's comments on the educational community hearkened back to the discussion on transactional distance, as well as a real need for open communication among all stakeholders.

Daisy described the community aspect of learning as a "trickle-down effect." She also discussed the idea that much of the weight of the responsibility in the virtual middle school environment is being shouldered by the teachers. Daisy shared:

Well, it's just a trickle-down effect. Obviously, there's the state that requires the standards and everything that we have to provide these kids. Then we also have to support the learning coaches. Some of these learning coaches are not, I hate to say it, but they're not extremely educated, but we have to help them as well and encourage the students and keep our morale up and keep our motivation and all of it and make sure we're prepared for the lessons, make sure we're trying to be as creative as possible and try to promote a good learning atmosphere. So, it's a hierarchy obviously, and we can only do so much.

The parents really have to enforce that ethic in their kids as well to be able to learn or even want to learn. So, it has a lot to do with . . . it could be a cultural thing too, where it's not really required as much. It just depends. It totally depends on family dynamic. We can do as much as we can do. State requires specific things. The school requires specific things. It's a huge effort on all of our part to get these kids to learn.

The other participants of this study pointed to teachers working with families and school administration working with teachers to motivate or discipline students accordingly. Still, regardless of the action taken by the members of the community to assist in student learning, the community of inquiry was found to be important to the overall success of the student.

The virtual environment can be isolating and lonely; thus, the participants each shared a real need for the nurturing of a supporting web of educational stakeholders. When teachers are viewed as supportive and caring humans, and when those teachers can call a student's family their teammates, it is much easier to establish meaningful and productive teacher-student relationships in the virtual middle school classroom.

THE CRUCIAL ELEMENTS OF THE VIRTUAL EDUCATIONAL COMMUNITY

Community is a vital element to all models of education. Regardless of the model, each educational stakeholder plays a different but crucial role in student success. The educational community is especially significant in the virtual environment, as the transactional distance between teachers and students is notably wider than it is in that of a brick-and-mortar school setting. In the case of the virtual classroom, community is key to student success.

The community of inquiry theoretical framework was utilized here, as the focus on community and educational relationships in virtual environments is central to student success in the virtual environment, as well as in the building of meaningful and productive teacher-student relationships.

The participants in this study each shared stories of working to build the virtual class community. Joy, Bobbi, Michelle, Mike, Jill, Karen, and Daisy each shared concrete examples of creating opportunities for community building in the virtual environment. These actions included deliberate and consistent interaction with students and the families of students during conferences. The participants' viewing of the class as a "team" or a "family" was a notable element observed in each of the stories of the participants in this study, including Tammy.

Each teacher understood and discussed the importance of connecting not only to the student but also to those who care about the student. It is in this communication with not only the student but also the student's support team that a teacher may build meaningful and productive relationships with students. At times, the only method of communication with a family is through text message, as recently, fewer people are checking or responding to emails or answering their phones. This is a reality of a trend in modern communication that we must realize and embrace if we are to build strong relationships with families.

Joy and Karen shared the belief that the educational community should apply to everyone in the local community, including not only the student's family but also every single person in the community. When asked to identify the members of the educational community, Joy stated: "Everybody is. Every single person is. There's rings, right? It goes out kind of like dropping a stone into the pond. It ripples out." Similarly, Karen pinpointed members of the educational community when she stated: "community members, churches, local businesses . . . people working at the grocery store. . . ."

The idea behind the inclusion of community members was one of unity and the greater good. Other participants mainly pointed to the student, the family, the teacher, and the school administration as the core of the middle school educational community. Tammy put a lot of faith in camera use for the establishment of a community, stating that it is important for her to see facial expressions of students and for the students to see one another. Tammy stated that she didn't view camera use much differently than she did in-person interaction, stating: "Suppose we were on the street or in my regular classroom talking, you wouldn't put a cover over your head while we're talking, right? There would be both a visual and an auditory exchange." However, she did not extend much beyond academics in discussing the construction of a thriving educational community.

The participants in the study identified those they believed to have vital roles in nurturing student success, while placing an emphasis on the importance of community in the virtual environment.

The participants also just simply understood the importance of engaging the educational community, especially in the virtual environment, where in-person interaction is a rare, if ever, occurrence. Much like the idea behind community of inquiry, the goal of community building and nurturing is in the facilitation of better learning through placing a heightened degree of importance on the procedures regarding instructional and social discussions, which ultimately lead to academic engagement.[3] Here again, the literature supports the findings of the participants.

The literature on the cruciality of the educational community supported the narratives of the teachers interviewed for this study. In connecting the educational community to teacher presence, the research supported the idea that essential community of inquiry depends on the teaching presence displayed in the classroom, stating that the formation of academic and social presence depends largely on the teaching presence.[4]

To be successful, students need to feel involved not only in their roles as students but also in the greater educational community. They also need to be able to identify that community. The identification of an encouraging educational community of inquiry is needed for meaningful and productive teacher-student relationships to develop. Students who believe themselves to be contributing, accepted, and respected members of the learning community have shown a lowered risk of dropping out of school.[5]

Ultimately, to be successful, a student needs to be able to identify specific members of an educational community that they trust. The task of reaching out and bringing together the members of the educational community often falls to the teacher. This unifying communication is especially important when working in the virtual environment, as the increased transactional distance of the model can be isolating to the student. The educational community needs to be trusted, accessible, and identifiable to the student, as well as being proactively involved with the student.

FROM THE PD!

Teacher feedback on the educational community:

Who Is in the Educational Community?

> All of us
> students, teachers, admin
> Everyone here
> me
> family, students, teacher, all the support people!
> VIVA, family
> Parents, LC
> teachers and parents
> parents, students, teachers
> Teacher, classmates, admin, etc.
> students, teachers, family
> Student, Teacher, family, admin, siblings
> parents, teachers, admin
> Yes, all of us
> teacher, parent, student
> Teacher, learning coach, peers
> family, teachers, students, admin
> All stakeholders
> Everyone at the school and their family
> siblings too
> me, students, parents, admin
> all of us, the LC, tutors, family
> family, teachers, students, classmates, admin
> support staff, classmates
> classmates
> administrators
> Everyone who has an influence on the student
> board members too

How Do the Family Members Interact with the Teachers?

> I can't stand when I hear a parent say "they are just here because they have to be/ we just have to get through it." . . . I hear it more and more often that parents don't see value in education.

For some of our students on the poverty line, many parents are more focused on daily survival and place school as a secondary priority.

THE EDUCATIONAL COMMUNITY AND TEACHING GOALS

The educational community, whether considered to be simply the teacher, student, and parent or thought to be the entire community from student to local, state, and federal governments, needs to be identifiable to the student as the student's web of support. The student should feel comfortable reaching out to the members of the educational community for assistance as needed, and the members of that community should understand their roles and embrace the challenges of the student. Does this always happen? Clearly not. But, if we aim high and fall a little short, it's better than never having taken the shot.

Each participant in this study discussed the educational community. When asked about the members of the educational community in the virtual environment, the teachers shared that the community includes the student, the teacher, and the learning coach. Some of the teachers went further, stating that other family members of the student should be included in the discussion of community. Expanding on this idea, other teachers in this study extended the web of community to include local businesses, society in general, and local and federal government agencies as crucial parts of the educational community. The educational community was viewed as greatly important to most students, as it encompasses the student's sphere of direct influence.

NOTES

1. Orthner, D. K., Jones-Sanpei, H., Akos, P., & Rose, R. A. (2013). Improving middle school student engagement through career-relevant instruction in the core curriculum. *Journal of Educational Research, 106*(1), 27–38.

2. Beck M., & Malley J. (2003). Pedagogy of belonging. *The International Child and Youth Care Network.* https://cyc-net.org/cyc-online/cycol-0303-belonging.html

3. Shea, P., & Bidjerano, T. (2009). Community of inquiry as a theoretical framework to foster "epistemic engagement" and "cognitive presence" in online education. *Computers & Education, 52*(3), 543–553.

4. Garrison, D. R., Anderson, T., & Archer, W. (2000). Critical inquiry in a text-based environment: Computer conferencing in higher education. *The Internet and Higher Education, 2*(2–3), 87–105.

5. Pendergast, D., Allen, J., McGregor, G., & Ronksley-Pavia, M. (2018). Engaging marginalized, "at-risk" middle-level students: a focus on the importance of a sense of belonging at school. *Education Sciences, 8*(3), 1–19.

Chapter 7

Literature on the Virtual Classroom in K–12 Settings

Families of K–12 students are drawn to virtual education for both personal and educational reasons, though a common underlying motive is a dissatisfaction of local brick-and-mortar schooling options. In discussing the reasons some families tend to seek out alternative schooling options, research has shown that, traditionally, K–12 teaching within the United States has been modeled in a one-size-fits-all structure, with little concern given for student individuality or differences in ability level.[1]

This shift to differentiated instruction has been deemed necessary, given the ever-increasing variation in student skills in modern classroom environments.[2] Thus, families who are seeking greater individualized instruction often turn to virtual schools, as this setting allows students to be homeschooled, online, by credentialed teachers, utilizing virtual classrooms.

While access to virtual K–12 classrooms has steadily increased in the last 20 years, much of the literature on virtual instruction has remained heavily skewed to postsecondary settings. However, research shows that K–12 virtual education is growing. By 2015, the number of K–12 students enrolled in at least one virtual classroom had grown to five million with close to 300,000 U.S. K–12 students enrolled in full-time online schools during the 2013–2014 school year.[3]

Further, many states have begun to require at least one virtual course be included in standard K–12 curriculum.[4] Still, the literature on virtual instruction has continued to focus on postsecondary students. Hopefully, the research in this study has worked to reduce that gap in the literature.

NOTES

1. Adkins, D., & Guerreiro, M. (2018). Learning styles: Considerations for technology enhanced item design. *British Journal of Educational Technology, 49*(3), 574–583.
2. Subban, P. (2006). A research basis supporting differentiated instruction. *International Education Journal, 7*(7), 935–947.
3. Samuelsohn, D., Merisotis, J., Grunwald, M., Crow, M., Dabars, W., & Remondi, J. (2015, September 23). Virtual schools are booming. Who's paying attention? *Politico.* www.politico.com/agenda/story/2015/09/virtual-schools-education-000227
4. Molnar, A., Miron, G., Elgeberi, N., Barbour, M. K., Huerta, L., Shafer, S. R., & Rice, J. K. (2019). *Virtual schools in the U.S. 2019.* National Education Policy Center. http://nepc.colorado.edu/publication/virtual-schools-annual-2019

Chapter 8

That One Student

As the teachers in this study discussed teacher presence, student safety, transactional distance, and the educational community, another common theme emerged, unprompted. Some of the teachers discussed, "that one student." To the participants, that one student was either a story of pride, a story of a missed opportunity, or a story of sadness. This was powerful, as it was unplanned and took me by surprise.

Each narrative was tied to the building of meaningful and productive teacher-student relationships and was important enough for each teacher to remember and to bring up during this study. The stories are independent, but all relate back to the research question: The purpose of this narrative inquiry study was to better understand the ways in which virtual middle school teachers build meaningful and productive relationships with their virtual students.

As the participants of this study spoke, most brought up a student who, for one reason or another, was memorable. Some of these narratives were stories of success, in which the teacher had facilitated student success in one form or another.

These stories shared teaching techniques and gave illustrations of social presence brought to life through concrete examples of the nurturing of student success. Other stories, however, were replete with sorrow and disappointment. Each of these stories acts as a reminder of the fact that students are individuals and not all of them respond to even the best strategies a good teacher has to offer. Still, planned teacher social presence was viewed as a typically reliable antidote for poor participation and lower than expected grades.

The teachers interviewed for this study have each taught in the virtual environment for at least 3 years and have accumulated a great deal of experience. This experience was shared through the storytelling of the teachers. As this was a personal narrative study, each teacher was free to tell uninterrupted stories. The anonymity of the teachers also provided further freedom to be open and honest. This inhibition allowed for free expression and storytelling.

The participants in this study told stories of triumph, heartbreak, and frustration. Encouraged by successes and learning from frustrations, each teacher continues to move forward, advancing the best teaching and interpersonal techniques available to them. For it is in these practices that meaningful and productive teacher-student relationships may be built.

THAT ONE STUDENT THE TEACHERS COULD NOT FORGET

Bobbi, Michelle, Mike, Joy, Jill, and Karen each offered at least one story of a student who was memorable for reasons or feelings of pride, disappointment, sadness, or triumph. In each case, the teachers spoke passionately. It is important to note that this finding emerged unprompted as independent stories were told by the participants in this study.

These stories of memorable students were offered as extensions of the other strands of focus. While the literature utilized in this study includes stories of individuals, most of the literature paints a broader picture, pointing to overall trends. The common thread discovered in this finding surprised me, as it was unanticipated. Still, the near ubiquity of the concept, now known to me as *That One Student* forced its way into the findings.

Teacher Input on "That One Student"

Bobbi shared the story of a student going through multiple hardships. Her story spoke to student needs beyond those academic in nature. She shared:

> I have a student this year who became homeless. Obviously, I did all the referrals for him but then it turns out that actually the root of the issue is I think his grandmother is mentally ill and he and his mom were living with them, but then the mom is now on drugs and the kid's just floating around. He is such a great kid. They're all great, right? But he's really tried to form a connection with me, which I appreciate, but then the point of the story is he keeps saying things like: "I'm so sorry, Mrs. C. I just can't focus on my class. I haven't heard from my mom in two days." I'm like: "Look, of course you can't focus on class." He's worried out of his mind with adult stuff that he shouldn't have to worry about, and he can't help it. And, his mom can't help it, and I hope she gets herself fixed, but at the end of the day I really do think it's very hard to ask these kids to come to school and learn when there's such crazy stuff going on in their house that they can't think.
>
> I think the Maslow's Hierarchy of Needs is super applicable. He doesn't know where he's going to be sleeping. He was in a shelter for youth for a while because they wouldn't let him go to the women's shelter because he's 13. He

doesn't know where his next meal's coming from, where his next bed's coming from, and he's still showing up to math class every day but then he's saying: "I'm really sorry I failed the quiz. I'm really sorry I turned this in late." I get it. And yet, my job is still to make sure he gets educated.

In this situation, the student might not pass his coursework, but he knows that his virtual teacher is there to support him. Because of this support, he is doing the best he can, given his situation. Bobbie included the dichotomy that the student should not be held to the same educational standards as a student with a stable home life but, at the same time, recognized that it is her job to teach him and see that he succeeds. On the flipside of that story, Bobbi shared a narrative of success.

> I just got an email from this student I had last year. . . . he would always come into class, and he was trying to teach himself German, which I don't speak great, but at least I can speak it. So, he would always come in and say something in German, so I would always answer him in German. And he just sent me an email and he's like: "Hey, I just wanted to tell you. I was going through my emails and you were a really cool science teacher." I was so happy because I felt like the connection worked. . . . we really had to chase him because when March rolled around, he dropped off and he had just been such a good student. I told Joanna, I was like: "I'll call him because I think this kid is really awesome and I think he'll respond." And he started coming back, and I was really happy about that, and he said this year he loves math and science, but English is really hard. I really want kids to get to high school and still stay in touch, and I tell them that all the time but really only a few do. You know?

Each of these stories was important enough for Bobbi to include in our discussion. These are stories that will stick with her, informing future teacher-student relationships.

Like Bobbi's second story, Karen shared a story of the triumph of making a strong connection with a student who needed assistance with working in the virtual environment. Karen shared:

> There was one student in particular last year that was kind of a handful in class. I think most of the time he was really bored, and it turned out that he just was kind of on a different intellectual level than his peers. So, he wasn't really building good relationships with his peers. But I started talking to him. We started talking about some different books. I started recommending books and stuff to him. And I feel like his whole classroom demeanor changed because he was getting attention from me and he didn't get that negative attention from his peers, where he was kind of being a little rude to them because he had a different sense of humor and just didn't connect to them on an intellectual level.

So, I felt like that's a good example of building a relationship with a student online where it was kind of in a positive way because it started off as really negative, and then once he started getting his attention in a more positive outlet, I was able to switch the way he was behaving with his peers as well.

Here again, the stress is placed on the human connection and teacher social presence. It was those two components of the teacher-student relationship that nurtured a successful outcome. Similar to Karen's narrative of success, Michelle shared a story of assisting an anxiety-stricken student from struggle to success. Michelle shared:

One of my students, I ended up talking with this mom. She came here because . . . school had been such an anxiety trigger. The student was throwing up every day because she had to go to school. Again, this was my first year here. . . . so, working with her, she would just answer questions, ask questions in private chat. She could email me. [I told her] I won't say who asked the question.

People are always trying to modify participation for her. Once we had that conversation, it became a little more calm and she began to participate a little bit more, to the point where I knew, second semester or whatever, she would always raise her hand to read, always wanting to participate. She ended up becoming one of my leaders in the class, and . . . her mom told me later on that year: "she's a whole different kid."

Here, Michelle employed social presence to assist with an anxiety-stricken student's needs. Michelle's incremental approach to fostering student participation paid huge dividends, as she aided in the student's journey, which took the student from hiding, while viewing school as a scary thing, to becoming a class leader and embracing Michelle's virtual environment.

Like Michelle, Jill shared the story of a student who also would not engage publicly but who succeeded due to teacher social presence. Jill shared:

[T]here's a student that I have right now who cannot . . . She just can't talk to them. She has a really hard time doing it on chat. So, what she'll do is in private chat. So, Miss, can you share without me? And I do, and I don't call her out. I will call her name as the name, I call the name like, thank you so much for XYZ for students who have participated or answered those questions. Great insight.

Acknowledging a correct answer, even if only given in a private chat, has proven to be a successful tool in building student confidence, creating a safe space, and nurturing student sense of belonging. Mike's and Michelle's stories are similar. In each case the student blossomed from being a hidden spectator to becoming a class leader. Mike shared:

> The other day, yesterday, I got an email from a student from last year on how I was doing and had some questions about if I had any students this year that were interested in K-pop. That in itself, just the fact that the student did something like that, shows that you can build a bond with a student through a virtual environment. . . . actually, when I got her, she was a student that was not really engaged. She really didn't care about school, and she struggled with it. The motivation wasn't there. I want to say it took me about two, three months to actually build a rapport with her, and have, just, a discussion. It has nothing do with actual schooling. I think in her case she was really into K-pop, so we started talking about that. Over time, what I noticed, what happened through the years, is she started engaging more. She'd read at the last class. It just built . . . I think I got an email over the summer or at the beginning of the school year, and this is, I think, my second or third email from her. But, again, it's one of those things where, and I think I mentioned it in my response to her, was how proud I am of her for turning into a student who could care less about school to trying really, really hard.
>
> I want to say she probably finished up with Bs, in that category, where it was really the effort that went behind it because I wasn't getting the effort at the beginning of the school year.

In his recount of the story, Mike explicitly stated that this success had: "nothing to do with actual schooling." Again, we see an example of teacher social presence, which led to a student knowing she had been seen and appreciated. Mike's efforts, ultimately, made all the difference.

Many of the narratives told here were told with pride. However, not all the stories ended in success and happiness. Joy found that great effort and stellar teacher presence are not always enough, as she shared a story of frustration and sadness. Joy shared:

> I think about one student I was convinced we were going to have a light bulb moment, and she had so much trauma in her past and I was really trying to make this connection with her about how things were going to get better. And I drove two hours on a weekend once a month each way to have coffee with her at a Starbucks just to let her know she wasn't alone because she had a traumatic home life. And so, I was trying so hard to make this connection with her . . . and she was brilliant, she still is, but I was just thinking: "man there's going to be this light bulb moment and all these F's are going to magically turn into A's and she's going to be like my most improved student. It's going to be amazing." And it never came, and she was just comfortable failing. I recognize her tactics, that she was just trying to survive, and that's totally acceptable. But I didn't get the connection emotionally either.
>
> There wasn't this big unloading of like we've made this connection over here, maybe it didn't happen academically but here socially, emotionally; we're connecting on this level. It was really unsatisfying, and it still bothers me.

As the participants discussed that one student, it became clear that teacher social presence was the tactic most often implemented to get students engaged, participating, back on track, and ultimately, successful in class. Overall, while teacher social presence didn't always produce honor-roll students, it did instill in the children a sense of care that the teacher felt for the student. This is the cornerstone of meaningful and productive teacher-student relationships.

Personally, I have found teacher social presence to be the deciding factor in student success, more so than almost any other aspect of teaching that I, more or less, have the ability to control. It seems as though I have a new *that one student* each year. As I think back, a few specific students stand out. I will change the names here.

James

James was a sixth-grade student of mine a few years back. He had an individualized education plan (IEP). His was a processing issue.

Here's a quick aside. When looking at students with processing issues, it is important to keep in mind that they often have plenty of cognitive ability, but it takes a little longer for them to arrive at an answer. In explaining processing issues to me, back in my college days, someone once told me to take out a piece of paper and pen and write down a list of everything I see in a room, and to stop after 60 seconds; then, to go into a different room and do it again, but this time write everything backwards. It was illuminating to me to see the size of each list. Obviously, my backward list was much shorter than my normal, forward list. The thing is, I hadn't lost any intelligence between lists. It just took me longer to write my second list due to my newly acquired processing issue.

Ok, back to James. James's mother had asked me to help him with a particular spelling issue with which he was struggling. As I worked with James, I saw his kind demeanor turn to one of subdued embarrassment. He was embarrassed and quiet because he was having an issue with his spelling. I picked up on this and told him to remember that he was smart and that nearly everyone had dealt with some kind of issue at some point. The difference was that he was actually doing something to help himself crack his particular challenge.

I told James about my absolute feeling of dread regarding biology and how I squeaked by with B's in college. It didn't mean I was dumb. It meant there was something that didn't come naturally to me. . . . and that's ok. James ended up nominating me for the California Pioneer Teacher of the Year award from the National Coalition for Public School Options, which I ultimately won. In his nomination, he didn't state that he was a great speller because of me. But he did say that because of me, he knew he wasn't dumb. I'll take that answer all day long over an A in spelling. James is now a college graduate.

Susie

Susie was a fairly recent sixth-grade student of mine. One day, during class, she was messaging her friends and told them that she was really down and upset. I called her mom to see if she was OK. Her mom said that she was behind in Math and was working to better her situation and that she would be OK. Susie and her mother personally thanked me for calling. Susie told her mom that my call showed that I was a good teacher. Again, she didn't say: "I'm really good at fractions because he's a good teacher." Her basis for her comment was the fact that I had cared enough to call.

Kristine

As discussed previously, the emergence of that one student does not always end in happiness. Kristine was a smart, talented sixth grader. Her test scores were high, and she was quick to answer questions in live classes. Her answers were usually correct. However, she consistently earned D's and F's. It really didn't seem to bother her. I worked with her mother and with VIVA admin to try to get her to complete missing work, but it never happened. She ended up with D's and F's. At the end of the year, she thanked me for my patience but stopped short of owning the disparity that was evident in her ability and her performance. Teacher social presence does not always show immediate results. But, maybe, partially because of some of my efforts, she realized some of her potential a few years later. I don't honestly know.

Connie

Every year, I seem to get a Connie; a student who succeeds without any participation. Connie was a student in my sixth-grade class a few years back. Connie's mother told me that she was competitive in the equestrian circuit and would not be attending many live classes because of her schedule. I told her that we would have to see how everything went before I could agree to these terms. I rarely saw Connie in class. I had to work with her a few times to ensure that a parent was not completing her work. But I quickly learned that she was earning her grades legitimately. It was clear that she understood the material. She earned straight A's without participating in our live sessions.

This brings forth an important point. As teachers, our ultimate goal is student success, both in the development of the whole child and academically. However, to some students, the academic component is not always a priority. To many teachers, this is a mind-blowing revelation, but it needs to be addressed. Overall, it has been found that our social presence helps in both the development of the whole child and with the academics of the child. Still, there is always that one student who just doesn't care about education and whose parents do nothing to encourage academic success. This is a hard pill to swallow, but it is, at times, a reality.

Overall, teacher effort in utilizing social presence has been found to be helpful in the building of meaningful and productive teacher-student relationships with most students. The examples shared have shown the, usually, positive outcomes of teacher social outreach. If it doesn't always work, that's OK. Nothing always works. According to https://www.statmuse.com/ Hall of Famer, Michael Jordan missed 1,445 free throws in his stellar career. His career percentage was 83.5%, meaning he made far more free throws than he missed. When Jordan missed a free throw, did he sullenly say, "Well, I guess I'm just not good at free throws. I'll stop trying?" No. You are Michael Jordan here. That's what we have to keep in mind. We now know what usually works for students and we are good at it, when we put our minds to it. We have discovered that the thing that works is teacher social presence. If it doesn't work for all students, that's OK. We will keep doing all we can to reach those who are reachable.

FROM THE PD!

Teachers Discuss Students and Stories of Triumph, Heartbreak, and Frustration

Who is a student with whom you have worked hard and have really seen growth? Please give first name only.

Jayden
Derrick
Carl
Zak
Azaria
Omar
Heaven
Jake
Cole
Sasha
Drew
Landon

Omar
Adrian
Lucius
Tre'sean
Quentin
Oscar
Nick
Steven
Zaynab
Shrie
Christian
Ella
Mercy
Kylie
Ellie
Harrison
Nathan
Xvier
Rose
Valeria
BJ
Nathaniel
Milana
Asia
Michael
Dylan
Elijah
Brooke
Precious
Isaac
Jayden
Gen

Now, please give the first name of a student with whom you have really worked hard, but who did not ultimately succeed.

Milliana
Omar
Derion
Elijah
Nick
Chloe

Tom
Hailey
Gabriel
Isaac
Jason
DJ
too many
Mikayla
Philip
Jay
Kaitlyn
Da'Monae
Saesha
Iris
Jaleo
adagio
Sean, but he did send me a message years later to thank me for trying.
aww that's beautiful!
That doesn't mean that they aren't learning.
YES! It doesn't mean they're not learning!
Relationships matter more than grades.
It is amazing how there are some students that did appreciate you and you learn about it years later at a graduation or something.
agreed
Sometimes you are the seed but don't always see the fruits of your efforts.
Agreed!
I'm sure, like your student, she felt the positive impact of those meetings later in life.
I've had them name their dogs after me.

Conclusion

Teacher-student relationships in the middle-school virtual environment are harder to build and nurture than is the case in the brick-and-mortar school setting. However, these meaningful and productive relationships are, indeed, possible.

This study has examined the challenges related to building meaningful and productive teacher-student relationships in the virtual middle school environment. As this is a narrative inquiry study, each chapter brought to light the stories of the participants as they discussed their experiences. Those stories were then analyzed to discover common threads among teachers, as well as with the literature.

The common threads revealed themes and subthemes. The themes discovered here were concepts that were repeatedly mentioned by the participants as important to building meaningful and productive teacher-student relationships. Identified as themes in this study were the concepts of teacher social presence, teacher academic presence, student safety, student sense of belonging, transactional distance, the educational community, and *that one student* who stuck in the mind of each participant. Teachers shared challenges, successes, and failures, as well as discussing their action with regard to each given situation.

While each theme contributed to the interwoven ideas of the facilitation of student success, both academic and in terms of the whole child, teacher social presence was found to be at the heart of most of the discussed teacher-student interaction. Many of the participants' stories involved a teacher facilitating opportunities for participation or engagement of a student through means that were personal and not academic. However, academic presence was also shown to be vital to student academic success. As teachers cannot interact with students only academically, teachers also cannot interact only socially with students.

Most of the participants in this study shared that they typically plan for teaching presence, as it is not as easy to be present in a virtual setting as it is in a brick-and mortar setting. A significant element of enhanced teacher presence was the idea that it is impossible for a student to succeed when that student does not feel safe in the virtual school environment. Safety here means safety to participate in class without fear of disrespect or ridicule.

Teachers in this study each discussed ways in which they work to foster a safe learning environment for all students. Encouragement of teamwork, supportive private chats, reassuring calls to home, caring emails, and inspiring texts sent to students were each mentioned as ways to create a safe learning environment. In this study, the feat of nurturing meaningful and productive teacher-student relationships was often mentioned as a direct result of teacher social and academic presence, (mainly social) both planned and spontaneous.

Ultimately, five main findings emerged. Through those findings, the recommendations that developed from the study were: (1) Deliberate teacher presence, especially social presence, should be taught to and implemented as a planning tool by teachers in the virtual environment. (2) Teachers need to focus on fostering students' sense of belonging in the virtual environment. (3) Virtual teachers should be required to learn about and then be taught strategies to better work toward bridging the gaps in the transactional distance found in the virtual environment. (4) Teachers and administrators should work with students and families in recognizing and connecting with the crucial members of the virtual educational community. (5) Teachers should be allowed time and opportunities to openly share stories and ideas regarding that one student they could not forget.

Teachers in this study gave many examples of the effectiveness of working outside of business hours, sending and receiving private messages and texts from students, taking an interest in students personally, and allowing students to see them as humans and not just as authority figures. Understandably, this concept could be intimidating to many teachers. However, if collegial conversations were to lead to ideas that could potentially expand the accessibility of teachers to students, even a little, it would be worth a few minutes of a professional development to have the discussions, as those personal connections have been found to be effective in the building of meaningful and productive teacher-student relationships, especially in virtual settings.

One last finding that was interwoven among the other findings was the idea that the use of cameras was found to be essential in the building of productive and meaningful teacher-student relationships in virtual settings. This finding highlighted the importance of teachers utilizing cameras as often as possible. Teachers really find it helpful to see each student, as actually looking at the students, even on camera, allows for a better understanding of a student's body language, gestures, and facial expressions. Also, the use of cameras allows for a glance into the student's home life.

It is not unusual for a student's camera to reveal a younger sibling on the lap of a student. This has happened more than once in my classes. This kind of student information is helpful, as it provides a deeper understanding into the atmosphere of the home and potential challenges for the student as they work from home. Ultimately, meaningful and productive teacher-student relationships in the virtual classroom setting depend on the effort and deliberate attention the teacher brings to the planning and execution of daily teaching and social communication with students. It is through the execution of this planning that a better understanding of student needs and challenges emerges and can be addressed.

VIVA is a virtual school that has utilized a virtual platform for 21 years. When the COVID-19 pandemic began to affect schools, VIVA did not change its methods. As many other schools struggled to make needed adjustments to emulate a brick-and-mortar setting, virtually, VIVA maintained its usual practice. However, the COVID-19 pandemic brought to light the idea that brick-and-mortar schools should be prepared for the next potential school-affecting event.

If brick-and-mortar school administrators were to train their teachers in the transferable ideas of teacher presence, fostering students' sense of belonging, learning about transactional distance and identifying a student's educational community, those schools would be better prepared to handle the next major event that could affect education and the educational model.

In sharing their takeaways from our conversations, the participants were asked to reflect not only on what was discussed but also to consider what they had learned in their time as virtual teachers that might be helpful to other virtual teachers. Ultimately, the participants discussed the necessary steps in building meaningful and productive teacher-student relationships in virtual environments. Along these lines, Daisy shared:

> There's a lot that you have to do to build a relationship. . . . I mean, that's a big question. I mean, that's a huge part of what we do, obviously. Not just teaching them. We have to have that relationship prior, or not prior, but build that relationship in order for them to learn and want to come to class.

In discussing the main points of the study, Joy, once again, shared her Sherpa analogy.

> We are like the Sherpa, we're the ones who know the path and we're supposed to be teaching them how to find it.

In discussing the big ideas, Mike shared:

I think what I've learned is that that relationship is possible. I don't think I fully understood that, even accepting the job of being a virtual teacher. You get used to interacting and talking with a group of students, and again, it's interesting because not every student shows up to school each day, at least, shows up to your class each day.

But what I have noticed is that it is possible to build a relationship with a student in a virtual environment. The question ends up being, how many of your students can you build that relationship with where you actually get a sense that the relationship is two-way, not just one-way?

In the end it is possible to build meaningful and productive teacher-student relationships in virtual middle-school classroom environments.

Here's one more piece from the PD. I hope it helps!

FROM THE PD!

What is a site you use, outside of the online school, to work with your students?

Jamboard
Padlet
Blooket
Kahoot
Quizziz
Khan Academy
whiteboard.fi
Nearpod
Google Classroom

I hope this book has been helpful to you in furthering and, possibly in defining, your professional goals.

Appendix A
Participant Recruitment: Virtual Middle-School Teachers

Seeking Volunteers

I am seeking volunteers to take part in a research study focused on the building of meaningful and productive relationships with virtual K–12 students in a virtual environment.

    The study is part of my Doctor of Education program at Northeastern University and is being conducted with oversight of Northeastern University's Institutional Review Board. This is my student research.

    The purpose of this study is to better understand the ways in which virtual K–12 teachers build meaningful and productive relationships with their virtual students.

    I am seeking virtual middle-school teachers with three years of experience teaching in virtual classrooms, who also have experience in brick-and-mortar settings. If you volunteer to take part in this study, you will be asked to participate in two interviews with me. The first interview will last approximately one hour. The second interview will last around 30 minutes. I will ask you questions about your experiences teaching in the K–12 virtual environment. Participation is entirely voluntary.

    If you wish to participate, please contact me at baker.n@northeastern.edu to arrange a time and place that works for you for the first interview.

Thanks!
Nicholas M. Baker

Bibliography

Adkins, D., & Guerreiro, M. (2018). Learning styles: Considerations for technology enhanced item design. *British Journal of Educational Technology, 49*(3), 574–583.

Akyol, Z., & Garrison, D. R. (2011). Assessing metacognition in an online community of inquiry. *The Internet and Higher Education, 14*(3), 183–190.

Alexander, K. L., Entwisle, D. R., & Horsey, C. S. (1997). From first grade forward: Early foundations of high school dropout. *Sociology of Education, 70*, 87–107.

Alley, K. M. (2019). Fostering middle school students' autonomy to support motivation and engagement. *Middle School Journal, 50*(3), 5–14.

Anderman, L. H. (2003). Academic and social perceptions as predictors of change in middle school students' sense of school belonging. *The Journal of Experimental Education, 72*, 5–22.

Anderson, T., Rourke, L. Garrison, R., & Archer, W. (2001). Assessing teaching presence in a computer conferencing context, *Journal of Asynchronous Learning Networks, 5*(2), 1–17.

Avery, K. F. G., Huggan, C. T., & Preston, J. P. (2018). The flipped classroom: High school student engagement through 21st century learning. *In Education, 24*(1), 4–21.

Baker, C. (2010). The impact of instructor immediacy and presence for online student affective learning, cognition, and motivation. *Journal of Educators Online, 7*(1), 1–30.

Baxter, J. (2012). Who am I and what keeps me going? Profiling the distance learning student in higher education. *International Review of Research in Open and Distance Learning, 13*(4), 108–129. https://doi.org/10.19173/irrodl.v13i4.1283

Beck, M., & Malley, J. (2003). Pedagogy of belonging. *The International Child and Youth Care Network*. https://cyc-net.org/cyc-online/cycol-0303-belonging.html

Bell, A. (2009). *Exploring Web 2.0: Second Generation Interactive Tools: Blogs, Podcasts, Wikis, Networking, Virtual Words, and More*. CreateSpace Independent Publishing Platform.

Bitzer, P., & Janson, A. (2014). Towards a holistic understanding of technology mediated learning services: A state-of-the-art analysis. In: European Conference on Information Systems (ECIS), Tel Aviv, Israel, Available at SSRN: https://ssrn

.com/abstract=2470946 *Proceedings of the European Conference on Information Systems* 1–20.

Blafanz, R., Fox, J., Bridgeland, J., & McNaught, M. (2009). *Grad nation: A guidebook to help communities tackle the dropout crisis.* America's Promise Alliance.

Bornt, D. (2011). *Moore's theory of transactional distance: Instructional design models, theories & methodology.* www.k3hamilton.com/LTech/transactional.html

Borup, J., Graham, C. R., &Velasquez, A. (2011). The use of asynchronous video communication to improve instructor immediacy and social presence in a blended learning environment. In A. Kitchenham, ed., *Blended learning across disciplines: Models for implementation* (pp. 38–57). IGI Global.

Chickering, A. W., & Gamson, Z. F. (1987). Seven principles for good practice in undergraduate education. *The Wingspread Journal, 9*(2), 3–7.

Collins, K., Grroff, S., Mathena, C., & Kupczynski, L. (2019). Asynchronous video and the development of instructor social presence and student engagement. *Turkish Online Journal of Distance Education, 20*(1), 53–70.

Cornell, D., Shukla, K., & Konold, T. R. (2016). Authoritative school climate and student academic engagement, grades, and aspirations in middle and high Schools. *AERA Open, 2*(2), 1–18.

Cox-Davenport, R. A. (2014). A grounded theory of faculty's use of humanization to create online course climate. *Journal of Holistic Nursing, 32*(1), 16–24.

Cranney, M., Wallace, L., Alexander, J. L., & Alfano, L. (2011). Instructor's discussion forum effort: Is it worth it? *MERLOT Journal of Online Learning and Teaching, 7*(3), 337–348.

Deci, E. L., & Ryan, R. M. (2008). Facilitating optimal motivation and psychological well-being across life's domains. *Canadian Psychology, 49*(1), 14–23.

Della Noce, D. J., Scheffel, D. L., & Lowry, M. (2014). Questions that get answered: The construction of instruction conversations on online asynchronous discussion boards. *Journal of Online Learning and Teaching, 10*(1), 80–96.

Dewey, J. (1933). *How we think.* Prometheus Books.

Dewey, J. (1938). *Education and experience.* Collier Books.

Dewey, J., & Bentley, A. (1949). *Knowing and the known.* Beacon Press.

Dikkers, A. G., Whiteside, A. L., & Lewis, S. (2013). Virtual high school teacher and student reactions to the social presence model. *Journal of Interactive Online Learning, 12*(3), 156–170.

Dixson, M. D. (2010). Creating effective student engagement in online courses: What do students find engaging? *Journal of the Scholarship of Teaching and Learning, 10*(2), 1–13.

Doda, N., & Knowles, T. (2008). Listening to the voices of young adolescents. *Middle School Journal, 39*(3), 26–33.

Dowshen, S. (2015). *Homeschooling (for kids).* The Nemours Foundation. www.kidshealth.org/en/kids/homeschool.html#:~:text=Parents%20choose%20to%20homeschool%20their,than%20the%20local%20school%20can

Durrington, V. A., Berryhill, A., & Swafford, J. (2006). Strategies for enhancing student interactivity in an online environment. *College Teaching, 54*(1), 190–193.

Dutton Tillery, A., Varjas, K., Meyers, J., & Collins, A. S. (2010). General education teachers' perceptions of behavior management and intervention strategies. *Journal of Positive Behavior Interventions, 12*(2), 86–102. https://doi.org/10.1177/1098300708330879

EducationData.org. (2020). *K–12 School Enrollment & Student Population Statistics.* https://educationdata.org/k12-enrollment-statistics

Ekmekci, O. (2013). Being there: Establishing presence in an online learning environment. *Higher Education Studies, 3*(1), 29–38. https://doi.org/10.5539/hes.v3n1p29

Eom, S. B., Wen, H. J., & Ashill, N. (2006). The determinants of students' perceived learning outcomes and satisfaction in university online education: An empirical investigation. Decision Sciences Journal of Innovative Education, 4(2), 215–235.

Estelami, H. (2017). The pedagogical and institutional impact of disruptive innovations in distance business education. *American Journal of Business Education, 10*(3), 97–108.

Eteokleous, N., Ktoridou, D., & Orphanou, M. (2014). Integrating wikis as educational tools for the development of a community of inquiry. *American Journal of Distance Education, 28*(2), 103–116.

Faust, P. B., Ennis, L. S., & Hodge, W. M. (2014). The relationship between middle grade student belonging and middle grade student performance. *Alabama Journal of Educational Leadership, 1*, 43–54.

Finn, J. D., & Rock, D. A. (1997). Academic success among students at-risk for school failure. *Journal of Applied Psychology, 82*, 221–234.

Forte, G., Schwandt, D., Swayze, S., Butler, J., & Ashcraft, M. (2016). Distance education in the U.S.: A paradox. *Turkish Online Journal of Distance Education, 17*(3). http://doi.org/10.17718/tojde.95102

Fredricks, J. A., Blumenfeld, P. C., & Paris, A. H. (2004). School engagement: Potential of the concept, state of the evidence. *Review of Educational Research, 74*(1), 59–109.

Furtak, E. M., & Kunter, M. (2012). Effects of autonomy-supportive teaching on student learning and motivation. *Journal of Experimental Education, 80*(3), 284–316.

Garrison, D. (2017). *E-learning in the 21st century: A community of inquiry framework for research and practice*, 3rd ed. Routledge.

Garrison, D. R. (2000). Theoretical challenges for distance education in the 21st century: A shift from structural to transactional issues. *The International Review of Research in Open and Distributed Learning, 1*(1). https://doi.org/10.19173/irrodl.v1i1.2

Garrison, D. R., & Arbaugh, J. B. (2007). Researching the community of inquiry framework: Review, issues and future directions. *The Internet and Higher Education, 10*(3), 157–172.

Garrison, D. R., Anderson, T., & Archer, W. (1999). Critical inquiry in a text-based environment: Computer conferencing in higher education. *The Internet and Higher Education, 2*(2), 87–105.

Garrison, D. R., Anderson, T., & Archer, W. (2000). Critical inquiry in a text-based environment: Computer conferencing in higher education. *The Internet and Higher Education,* 2(2–3), 87–105.

Garrison, D. R., Anderson, T & Archer, W. (2001). Critical thinking, cognitive presence, and computer conferencing in distance education. *American Journal of Distance Education, 15*(1), 7–23. https://doi.org/10.1080/08923640109527071

Garrison, D. R., Anderson, T., & Archer, W. (2010). The first decade of the community of inquiry framework: A retrospective. *Internet and Higher Education, 13*(1–2), 5–9.

Goodenow, C. (1993). Classroom belonging among early adolescent students: Relationships to motivation and achievement. *The Journal of Early Adolescence, 13*(1), 21–43.

Gray, J. A., & DiLoreto, M. (2016). The effects of student engagement, student satisfaction, and perceived learning in online learning environments. *International Journal of Educational Leadership Preparation, 11*(1), n1.

Gunawardena, C. N., Lowe, C., & Anderson, T. (1997). Interaction analysis of a global online debate and the development of a constructivist interaction analysis model for computer conferencing. *Journal of Educational Computing Research, 17*, 395–429.

Harris, L. R. (2008). A phenomenographic investigation of teacher conceptions of student engagement in learning. *The Australian Educational Researcher, 35*(1), 57–79.

Hellmer, S. (2012). Student autonomy and peer learning: An example. *Högre Utbildning, 2*(1), 51–54.

Hoskins, B. J. (2012). Connections, engagement, and presence. *Journal of Continuing Higher Education, 60*(1), 51–53.

Jackson, L. C., Jones, S. J., & Rodriguez, R. C. (2010). Faculty actions that result in student satisfaction in online courses. *Journal of Asynchronous Learning Networks, 14*(4), 78–96.

Jackson, P., Cashmore, A., & Scott, J. (2010). *Sense of belonging: Background literature*. https://www2.le.ac.uk/offices/ssds/projects/student-retention-project/dissemination/papers-and-publications/Sense%20of%20Belonging%20Lit%20Review.docx

Jackson, S. H. (2019). Student questions: A path to engagement and social presence in the online classroom. *Journal of Educators Online, 16*(1), 1–8.

Jin, S. H. (2005). Analyzing student–student and student–instructor interaction through multiple communication tools in web-based learning. *International Journal of Instructional Media, 32*(1), 59–67.

K12 Inc. (2021). *School Mission*. https://www.k12.com/about-k12/company-mission.html

K12 Inc. (2022). *Over 1 million students have chosen public school at home with K12!* https://www.k12.com/about-k12/million-students.html

Kaufmann, R., Sellnow, D. D., & Frisby, B. N. (2015). The development and validation of the online learning climate scale (OLCS), *Communication Education, 65*(3), 307–321.

Ke, F. (2010). Examining online teaching, cognitive, and social presence for adult students. *Computers & Education, 55*, 808–820.

Ke, F., & Chavez, A. F. (2013). *Web-based teaching and learning across culture and age*. Springer.

Kehrwald, B. (2008). Understanding social presence in text-based online learning environments. *Distance Education, 29*(1), 89–106.

Kingsbury, I. (2020). *Online learning: How do brick and mortar schools stack up to virtual schools?* EdChoice. https://www.edchoice.org/wp-content/uploads/2020/09/09-20-Virtual-Schools-During-COVID-UPDATED-1.pdf

Kozan, K., & Richardson, J. C. (2014). Interrelationships between and among social, teaching and cognitive presence. *The Internet and Higher Education, 21*, 68–73.

Kranzow, J. (2013). Faculty leadership in online education: Structuring courses to impact student satisfaction and persistence. *MERLOT Journal of Online Learning and Teaching, 9*(1), 131–139.

Kucuk, S., & Richardson, J. C. (2019). A structural equation model of predictors of online learners' engagement and satisfaction. *Online Learning, 23*(2), 196–216.

Laborie, K., & Stone, T. (2015). *Interact and engage! 50+ activities for virtual training, meetings and webinars.* Association for Talent Development.

Lapadat, J. C. (2007). Discourse devices used to establish community, increase coherence, and negotiate agreement in an online university course. *The Journal of Distance Education, 21*(3), 59–92.

Leese, M. (2009). Out of class—out of mind? The use of a virtual learning environment to encourage student engagement in out of class activities. *British Journal of Educational Technology, 40*(1), 70–77.

Louwrens, N., & Hartnett, M. (2015). Student and teacher perceptions of online student engagement in an online middle school. *Journal of Open, Flexible and Distance Learning, 19*(1), 27–44.

Mandernach, B. J., Forrest, K. D., Babutzke, J. L., & Manker, L. R. (2009). The role of instructor interactivity in promoting critical thinking in online and face-to-face classrooms. *MERLOT Journal of Online Learning and Teaching, 5*(1), 49–62.

Marks, R. B., Sibley, S. D., & Arbaugh, J. B. (2005). A structural equation model of predictors for effective online learning. *Journal of Management Education, 29*(10), 531–563.

Maslow, A. (1962). *Toward a psychology of being.* Van Nostrand.

Meyer, K. A. (2014). J-B ASHE higher education report series (AEHE): Student Engagement Online: What Works and Why. *ASHE Higher Education Report, 40*(6), 1–15. Jossey-Bass.

Mohd Khalid, M. N., & Quick, D. (2016). Teaching presence influencing online students' course satisfaction at an institution of higher education. *International Education Studies, 9*(3), 62–70.

Molnar, A., Miron, G., Elgeberi, N., Barbour, M. K., Huerta, L., Shafer, S. R., & Rice, J.K. (2019). *Virtual schools in the U.S. 2019.* National Education Policy Center. http://nepc.colorado.edu/publication/virtual-schools-annual-2019

Moore, M. (1993). Theory of transactional distance. In D. Keegan, ed., *Theoretical Principles of Distance Education* (1st ed., pp. 22–38). Routledge.

Moore, M. (1997). Theory of transactional distance. In D. Keegan, ed., *Theoretical Principles of Distance Education* (2nd ed., pp. 22–38). Routledge.

Moore, M., & Kearsley, G. (1996). Distance education: A systems review. Wadsworth Publishing Company.

Moore, M. G. (1972). Learner autonomy: The second dimension of independent learning. *Convergence, 5*(2), 76–88.

Moore, M. G. (1973). Towards a theory of independent learning and teaching. *Journal of Higher Education, 44*, 661–679.

Murdock, T. B., Anderman, L. H., & Hodge, S. A. (2000). Middle-grade predictors of students' motivation and behavior in high school. *Journal of Adolescent Research, 15*, 327–351.

Nishikant, S. (2009). The paradigm shift for adult education: From educational slavery to learning freedom of human brain with synaptic learning. In T. Kidd, ed., *Online education and adult learning: New frontiers for teaching practices* (pp. 150–164). IGI Global.

Oliphant, T., & Branch-Mueller, J. (2016). Developing a sense of community and the online student experience. *Education for Information, 32*(4), 307–321.

Orcutt, J. M., & Dringus, L. P. (2017). Beyond being there: Practices that establish presence, engage students, and influence intellectual curiosity in structured online learning environment. *Online Learning, 21*(3), 15–35.

Orthner, D. K., Akos, P., Rose, R., Jones-Sanpei, H., Mercado, M., & Woolley, M. (2010). CareerStart: A middle school student engagement and academic achievement program. *Children and Schools, 32*, 223–234.

Orthner, D. K., Cook, P., Rose, R., & Randolph, K. A. (2002). Welfare reform, poverty, and children's performance in school: Challenges for the school community. *Children and Schools, 24*, 105–121.

Orthner, D. K., Jones-Sanpei, H., Akos, P., & Rose, R. A. (2013). Improving middle school student engagement through career-relevant instruction in the core curriculum. *Journal of Educational Research, 106*(1), 27–38.

Peacock, S., & Cowan, J. (2019). Promoting sense of belonging in online learning communities of inquiry in accredited courses. *Online Learning, 23*(2), 67–81.

Pendergast, D., Allen, J., McGregor, G., & Ronksley-Pavia, M. (2018). Engaging marginalized, "at-risk" middle-level students: a focus on the importance of a sense of belonging at school. *Education Sciences, 8*(3), 1–19.

Perry, J. C. (2008). School engagement among urban youth of color: Criterion pattern effects of vocational exploration and racial identity. *Journal of Career Development, 34*, 397–422.

Prothero, A., & Samuels, C. A. (2021, February 25). Home schooling is way up with COVID-19. Will it last? *Education Week.* www.edweek.org/policy-politics/home-schooling-is-way-up-with-covid-19-will-it-last/2020/11

Purarjomandlangrudi, A., Chen, D., & Nguyen, A. (2016). Investigating the drivers of student interaction and engagement in online courses: A study of state-of-the-art. *Informatics in Education, 15*(2), 269–286.

Ritter, M., & Lemke, K. (2000). Addressing "the seven principles for good practice in undergraduate education" with internet-enhanced education. *Journal of Geography in Higher Education, 24*(1), 100–108. http://doi.org/10.1080/03098260085171

Rowe, F., & Stewart, D. (2009). Promoting connectedness through whole school approaches: A qualitative study. *Health Education, 109*, 396–413.

Samuelsohn, D., Merisotis, J., Grunwald, M., Crow, M., Dabars, W., & Remondi, J. (2015, September 23). Virtual schools are booming. Who's paying attention? *Politico.* www.politico.com/agenda/story/2015/09/virtual-schools-education-000227

Shea, P., & Bidjerano, T. (2009). Community of inquiry as a theoretical framework to foster "epistemic engagement" and "cognitive presence" in online education. *Computers & Education, 52*(3), 543–553.

Steinberg, L. D., Brown, B. B., & Dornbush, S. M. (1996). *Beyond the classroom: Why school reform has failed and what parents need to do.* Simon and Schuster.

Strauss, V. (2020, March 27). 1.5 billion children around globe affected by school closure: What countries are doing to keep kids learning during pandemic. *The Washington Post.* www.washingtonpost.com/education/2020/03/26/nearly-14-billion-children-around-globe-are-out-school-heres-what-countries-are-doing-keep-kids-learning-during-pandemic/

Subban, P. (2006). A research basis supporting differentiated instruction. *International Education Journal, 7*(7), 935–947.

Swan, K. (2001). Virtual interaction: Design factors affecting student satisfaction and perceived learning in asynchronous online courses. *Distance Education, 22*(2), 306–331.

Thomas, L. (2012). *Building student engagement and belonging at a time of change in higher education.* Paul Hamlyn Foundation.

Toppin, I. N., & Toppin, S. M. (2016). Virtual schools: The changing landscape of K–12 education in the U.S. *Education and Information Technologies, 21*(6), 1571–1581.

Toshalis, E. (2015). *Make me! Understanding and engaging student resistance in school.* Harvard Educational Press.

Tovar, E., & Simon, M. A. (2010). Factorial structure and invariance analysis of the sense of belonging scales. *Measurement and Evaluation in Counseling and Development, 43*(3), 199–217.

Umbach, P. D., & Wawrzynski, M. R. (2005). Faculty do matter: The role of college faculty in student learning and engagement. *Research in Higher Education, 46*(2), 153–184. https://doi.org/10.1007/s11162-004-1598-1

Vaccaro, A., Daly-Cano, M., & Newman, B. M. (2015). A sense of belonging among college students with disabilities: An emergent theoretical model. *Journal of College Student Development, 56*(7), 670–686.

Wallace, T. L., & Sung, H. C. (2017). Student perceptions of autonomy-supportive instructional interactions in the middle grades. *Journal of Experimental Education, 85*(3), 425–449.

Wanstreet, C. E. (2009). Interaction in online learning environments. *The Perfect Online Course: Best Practices for Designing and Teaching, 7*(4), 399–411.

Whiteside, A. L. (2015). Introducing the social presence model to explore online and blended learning experiences. *Online Learning, 19*(2), 53–72.

Williams, R. S., & Humphrey, R. (2007). Understanding and fostering interaction in threaded discussion. *Journal of Asynchronous Learning Networks, 11*(2), 129–143.

Yazzie-Mintz, E. (2007). *Voices of students on engagement: A report on the 2006 High School Survey of Student Engagement.* Center for Evaluation & Educational Policy, Indiana University.

About the Author

Nicholas M. Baker, EdD, is a virtual sixth grade teacher with the Violetta Virtual Academies. He lives in Ventura County, California, with his wife, Marina, and daughter, Violetta. Dr. Baker has taught K–8 in the virtual setting for more than two decades and was the recipient of the National Coalition of Public School Options, California Teacher of the Year Award in 2009.

www.ingramcontent.com/pod-product-compliance
Lightning Source LLC
Chambersburg PA
CBHW032028230426
43671CB00005B/231